OUR GIFT

FROM THE GREATEST GENERATION

By
Robert Gilbert

Copyright © 2024

All Rights Reserved

ISBN:

Hardcover: 978-1-917327-08-4

Paperback: 978-1-917327-10-7

Ebook: 978-1-917327-09-1

DEDICATION

I want to dedicate this book to all the men and women who serve our country and those who have made the ultimate sacrifice.

Your selflessness, bravery, commitment, and, dedication to our country to protect our liberties and freedoms have given us OUR GIFT and will never be forgotten.

We Celebrate and Salute ALL THE HEROES.

ABOUT THE AUTHOR

Robert Gilbert was born and raised in Sebring, Florida, and grew up hearing backyard stories from his dad about his experiences in battle during WWII, his capture, and captivity. He found it fascinating as a child as will you when you read his stories. Robert felt compelled to write this book to document his father's journey and legacy so his story could serve as a reminder to honor the sacrifices of veterans and to preserve their stories for future generations, ensuring that the lessons of history are not forgotten. They gave us OUR GIFT- From The Greatest Generation.

ACKNOWLEDGMENT

I owe a great deal of thanks to my dad for taking time through the years to tell me these stories play-by-play. He had enough faith in me even at a very young age that he could tell me, knowing I could handle it. Dad knew that I needed to know the good, the bad, and the ugly sides of war. As I mentioned in "The Memory" chapter, it really was like he was right there writing this book alongside me. The writings and recordings he left behind are blessings, and when combined with the stories he told me, they take this book to a whole new level. The fact that this book is 100% true, raw history makes it incredibly intriguing.

My Mom deserves credit for writing some of these stories while my Dad narrated. Her handwriting was beautiful and easy to read. I want to thank my sister, Terri Gilbert Jordan, for her assistance in deciphering some of Dad's handwriting and being on hand for any questions that came up. I especially want to thank my girlfriend, Shelley Bonate, to who I owe a debt of gratitude for helping get this book from my thoughts to fruition and standing by my side through this entire process. Her typing up my hen scratch, extensive research, suggestions, and unwavering support and belief in me and my writings made this book possible. I could not have done it without her. Shelley's heart is in this book as well as mine, not only for my dad but for hers. Her dad was also a POW in WWII, captured at the Battle of the Bulge, and we share that strong sense of patriotism and pride for our country and for the sacrifices our fathers made for our freedoms. Our generation, who followed this Greatest Generation, have lived in the midst of their GREATNESS.

Staff Sergeant Roy A. Gilbert

United States Army – WWII

1943-1945

MILITARY ACHIEVEMENTS

Sergeant Gilbert served in the 3rd Army Division under the leadership of George S. Patton. He was wounded twice and awarded the Purple Heart with Oak Leaf Cluster, the European-African-Middle Eastern Campaign medal and Bar with 4 Bronze Stars, the Prisoner of War medal, WWII Liberty Medal, the US Army Good Conduct Medal & Ribbon Bar, Infantry Marksman Award, Sergeant 1st Class, Army Ground Forces, 35th Infantry Division Patch, 3rd Army Patch, Army Infantry School Patch.

TABLE OF CONTENTS

DEDICATION ii

ABOUT THE AUTHOR iii

ACKNOWLEDGMENT iv

MILITARY ACHIEVEMENTS vii

PREFACE x

WHAT TRIGGERED THE BOOK? xiii

1. THE MEMORY 1

2. DAD'S LIFE GROWING UP 3

3. DAD'S CHARACTER 5

4. PIANO STORY 11

5. THE RAILROAD 14

6. REBEL 16

7. THE PURPLE HEART 20

8. WHEN HEAVEN APPEARS IN HELL 22

9. TRAGEDY IN THE TRENCHES 25

10. TWO VERSIONS OF DAD 31

11. THE FARMHOUSE AND MOST PERSONAL KILL 34

12. THE CAPTURE AND INTERROGATION 39

13. TWILIGHT ZONE MOMENTS 45

14. DAD'S MIRACLE BIBLE 46

15. CHRISTMAS EVE THROUGH THE EYES OF A POW ... 49

16. DEATH MARCH TO SANDBOSTEL, GERMANY 55

17. THE INTERVIEW 1992 60
18. THE LIBERTY SHIP HOMECOMING 82
19. FROM HELL TO HEAVEN 88
20. PHONE CALL THAT ANSWERED MANY PRAYERS .89
21. WHAT REALLY HAPPENED TO REBEL 91
22. POST-WAR 94
23. HITTING THE DECK - SIX FLAGS 99
24. GENERAL PATTON: A LEGACY OF LEADERSHIP ...101
25. LAST CHAPTER 108

PREFACE

Who should read this book? Everybody. Let's just say anyone who cares about the country they live in, what it stands for, and what it means to them. Do we not all want the same thing? We all want our liberties and freedoms, do we not? Freedom of speech, freedom of religion, and the security of living in peace with your family. Simply the freedom to basically do whatever you want in life, short of breaking the law.

A quote from the late Texas Republican, Sam Johnson, "Freedom has a taste to those who fight and almost die that the protected will never know." That quote really stuck in my head, so I wrote it down and put it on my refrigerator so I would never forget it. Do not feel guilty if you take our liberties and freedoms for granted, as they have been there since the day we were born. They were not called the Greatest Generation for nothing. Think about this. Most of them grew up in tough times when life was anything but a bed of roses. They grew up poor during that time period, The Great Depression. Many had to grow up faster than any kid should have to. My Dad was no exception. The teenage kids of that generation could have looked to their future with not much hope for a financially better way of life as there was simply a lack of opportunity. However, the one thing that everyone did have and probably took for granted, just like many of us these days, was our liberties and freedoms.

Suddenly, their way of life was facing a very real and present danger and sickening threat. After Pearl Harbor was attacked by the Japanese, it was made clear to all Americans that halfway around the world, a lunatic dictator, Adolf Hitler, wanted to take over all countries and rule the entire planet. The sleeping giant woke up. Everything they had grown to love about their country was on the line. After all, this was the United States of America, and UNITED they were. Just the thought of losing the liberties and freedoms that they've had all their lives was more than anyone could bear, and bear they did not.

The mindset of all was that this would NEVER happen to OUR country. At that time, if anyone took these rights for granted before, they were not now. While a World War was looming inevitably on the horizon, our country's Greatest Generation was in the infancy stages of EARNING that title. EVERYONE was on the same page. NO ONE questioned WHY, and NO ONE was going to take away their liberties and freedoms. Our people working together collectively ALL made the IMPOSSIBLE, POSSIBLE. The men enlisting had the support of the ENTIRE nation behind them. Though women did not go into combat at that time, they were ESSENTIAL in the nursing/medical field and worked alongside men in assembly lines in the factories, producing the gear and weapons to fight that war. They were the spokes in the wheel to keep it turning.

My Dad was ONE of 16 million American men who went off to fight that war. He was a sergeant in the 3rd Army under the leadership of General George Patton and was assigned to fight in the European theatre against the Germans. EVERYONE needs to know what it took from each man to win that war and hand us "Our Gift." The gift of preserving our liberties and freedoms. This book is a combination of stories he told me throughout the years, along with papers that I found my Dad had handwritten or typed in his later years, as well as ones my mom wrote for him as he recalled the stories. This, along with an actual tape recording of Dad's voice describing one particular incident, was a huge plus. As you read on, you will get to know my Dad, and he might just remind you of someone you know or have known in the past.

For the average person, reading these stories will be very enlightening as to what combat is really like. You veterans of all wars who saw combat will all get it. My Dad's stories contain EVERY emotion you can imagine. Fear, relief, joy, sadness, empathy, happiness, confusion, twilight-zone moments, and above all, spiritual moments. Two of his spiritual experiences will boost the most devout believer's faith. They are powerful enough to even make an atheist at least pause and maybe even wonder.

After countless hellish skirmishes and battles in Rhineland, Normandy, Northern France, and Central Europe (four major campaigns), Dad and his platoon, or what was left of them, were captured and now became prisoners of that war. Dad thought he had seen hell on the battlefield, but the next four months in the captivity of the Germans were worse. He witnessed true, raw evil on death marches and in concentration camps. He saw first-hand the horrors of evil they were stopping from coming to America.

At the end of this book, you will read a description of these four months in my Dad's own words. It's the most impactful writing I've ever read on any subject. I swear, I can't read parts of it to this day without tearing up. Although my Dad and countless others had experienced hell on earth, they also experienced heaven on earth in the end. Good conquered evil, and against all odds, my Dad was spared. There are parts of this book that are going to reach into the deepest parts of your soul and pull out emotions you didn't realize you had or maybe lost a long time ago. We all need this now more than any other time.

WHAT TRIGGERED THE BOOK?

It's funny how certain occurrences in life can slap you upside the head and trigger an immediate reaction in some form or another. This happened to me a few years ago, triggering the birth of this book. For about a week or two, I had been hearing a comment by one of our congresswomen that we were operating concentration camps on our southern border for those entering the United States illegally. The first time I heard that, I thought, 'Does she really believe that our detention centers are concentration camps?'

The times I heard it after that, I tuned it out as total BS and just too stupid to acknowledge. However, as I was walking through the house one night in the background on TV, I heard that dumb comment once again, and it hit me a little differently. I immediately either said to myself or out loud, "You have NO IDEA what a concentration camp is like!"

Suddenly, it was like I was put on autopilot and guided to a place where important papers are kept. This was when I pulled out Dad's page-and-a-half description from the time of his capture to the camps or internment camps we now know of as death or concentration camps that he experienced. After reading over that short page and a half, I realized why it had been so long since the last time I'd read it. It's just too damn depressing. I really can't be mad at the congresswoman who made that statement. She is simply clueless and uneducated, which is not entirely her fault. Unfortunately, she is the perfect example of how some of our educators are brainwashing or just not teaching the truth to our kids.

Something sparked in me that night. The next day, I could not stop thinking about all the war stories my Dad had told me throughout the years as I was growing up. At the same time, I felt a wave of anxiety come over me. I thought, "These stories are incredible, and I am the only one who knows them!"

If I *died* tomorrow, these stories would *die* with me. I felt overwhelmed that it would be a *sin* not to document them and share them with you.

1

THE MEMORY

The WWII stories my Dad told me were mesmerizing, to say the least. I heard most of them for the first time when I was very young before I was even in high school. Though the stories never changed, I never got tired of hearing them. Dad told me for two reasons. One, I asked, two, he knew, even at that age, I *needed* to know. I learned early on that the best time to talk to him was when he was doing something physical outside and he stopped for a water break under the shade of the trees in the backyard. In hindsight, I think the physical exertion "chilled" him out just enough to help him relax and tell me these stories.

Again, looking back, I think Dad needed this as much as I did. I sucked it all up like a sponge, and to this day, I can see the look in his eyes when he was back there. Certain stories I heard many times and other stories, or parts of them, I would not ask about again because even as a little kid, I could also tell by his eyes when it was best not to bring up certain incidences again. God, I cherish those times in the backyard now more than ever. I wish I had talked to him more as I got older, but things changed as life could just get in the way.

Before I began to document these stories, I couldn't help wondering how my memory would be after all these years. As I sat down to write the first story (The Railroad), it became apparent really quickly how easy it was going to be. Have you ever had a favorite movie that you watched several times over the years? I know that's rare for me too. However, some are so good you don't mind. Even though the story never changes, you can pick up small things you missed the first time. You can remember these movies for the rest of your life. That is exactly how my Dad's war stories are for me. I have visions of each one of these stories, and his voice is burned into my memory bank.

With each one of these stories, it was like I was watching a movie with my Dad narrating. Realize I am alone in the house I grew up in and that my Dad died in. The TV is on, but the sound is off, and I only have the sound of the fan, only white noise, so I can focus. I wrote all these stories at the dinner table just opposite where he sat in his wheelchair for years before he died. I told you writing these stories over time was easy, but it was also EXHAUSTING. I did not expect the emotional roller coaster they took me on. From the visions I have of these stories and my Dad telling them, I swear I felt like he was right there with me. That is why they came so easily. I could hear the tone of voice he had, I could see his facial expressions, and especially that 1,000-yard stare when his memories and mind's eye took him back to that place and time. Thanks, Dad for the help, I could not have done it alone.

2

DAD'S LIFE GROWING UP

My Dad, Roy Gilbert, was born in 1922 in Tennille, Georgia. His father died in 1927 of tuberculosis when he was only five years old. I was quite young when I asked my Dad if he remembered his Dad. When I asked, he gazed off and said, "Rob, I only have two memories about my daddy. He brought home a baby rabbit he had found abandoned and wanted William (his younger brother) and me to take care of. The only other memory I have is talking to him through a screen porch until his passing. We couldn't get close because of his TB." He didn't really have a childhood. He had to grow up fast. Just a few years after his dad died and he could handle a shovel, he dug graves as there was a shortage of men at that time. I remember Dad saying in his booming Georgia accent years ago, "I think I've buried every old woman in Tennille, Georgia." This went on for years until he left for the war. I remember Dad talking about him and his brother hunting a lot through the years and nothing they shot went to waste as it was simply a supplement to their diet. I wonder now what guidance Dad had as a kid growing up to go in the right direction. Nothing against Dad's mother, she was a fine Christian woman and I'm sure she had my dad and his brother in church EVERY Sunday. All of us kids grew up with her and none of us ever heard a bad word come out of her mouth about anything or anybody. I did hear Dad talk about "Papa" from time to time who was his mother's father. William A. Daniel. Mr. Daniel began his career in the pharmaceutical business in 1898 which was originally started by his uncle in 1885. Mr. Daniel, "Papa", ran a drug store in Tennille, Georgia. Dad said there was a soda fountain in part of the drug store for a short time before the war and he was the soda jerk. He would play music for the kids that would hang out there on certain nights of the week. The family operated this small store until early 1942 when Mr. Daniel died. Dad's mom then converted the business into a full-time sundry store and ran it throughout WWII when her sons, William and my dad, were called into service. At least they had this but times were still tough. Maybe Papa influenced my Dad because he did go to the University of Georgia College of Pharmacy after the war. Dad said, many times, "I was sure thankful for the GI bill, I couldn't have done it without it."

Dad's House Growing Up in Tennille, GA

3

DAD'S CHARACTER

Award Given to Roy Gilbert for his many contributions to his community.

I feel it is important that you get to know the type of person he was, from his moral character to his personality, before you walk in his shoes on the battlefield. There are plenty of stories of his experiences in WWII that will captivate you as they have me all my life. Looking back on it, I realize he was quite complex. As a young kid, I could not help but notice how people interacted with my Dad.

ROBERT GILBERT

He was a pharmacist by trade and the owner of Gilbert Drugs in Sebring, Florida. He was very active in the community in his younger years.

Dad was 37 when I was born. My earliest memories of my Dad are that he was tall, physically strong, and had a very soothing temperament when he talked to us, especially when we were ill. Not to take anything away from my mom, as we were blessed to have two of the greatest parents a kid could wish for. It's just when Dad would get home from work and come in the room you were laid up in ailing, you just knew everything was going to be okay. Whether the ailment required medication or not, it didn't matter, as it was his mere presence that did the most.

I think it was the feeling of love and security that did the trick. As a young kid, I rode with him to the drug store for after-hour calls at night. I remember the look on people's faces and the tone of their voices when they would meet up with Dad. I thought to myself, 'Yeah, I know that feeling.' Looking back on it, it was just simply that he had this aura about him. It especially shined when life was not kind to you and beating you up.

Dad had a natural way of making you feel better. My Dad was always religious, and what he experienced over there strengthened his faith. I know it has mine. Maybe he was spared to come back and serve the people of this town, whether it be as owner and pharmacist of Gilbert Drugs, serving on the Sebring City Council, Sebring Utilities Commission, Chamber of Commerce, Board of the Salvation Army and all kinds of drives for many years.

OUR GIFT

People of this town spoke highly of and grew to love my Dad because they knew he *really* cared about them and their families. He was always on call, and I remember him going downtown to fill a prescription all hours of the night and many times personally delivering them to the homes of the people who couldn't make it to the store. Oftentimes, it was for a child getting sick in the middle of the night, and my Dad had a very special place in his heart for sick kids.

After my Dad's death, the people of Sebring, Florida, who he served during his life, placed a plaque on the boardwalk at Highlands Hammock State Park in his honor. The plaque reads, "In Loving Memory of Dr. Roy Gilbert, A True Gentleman." And that he was.

ROBERT GILBERT

OUR GIFT

My Dad's generation is about gone, but all the comments I've heard through the years were things like, "Your father was sure good to us." "He sure was a fine man." "We sure miss your Dad." "He was a true gentleman." Or, "Lordy, I don't know what we would have done without your Daddy." That last line was from an elderly black woman, and the sincerity in her eyes really told the story. I felt it.

Just recently, I was in the grocery store and ran into a neighbor friend of mine. I told her about the book, and we briefly discussed how people felt about him. She said, "My preacher used to refer to your Dad as a Prince of a Man." I said, "Wow, I never heard that one."

What a great comment, especially from a well-respected preacher. You know, it took me until I was 60 years old to realize exactly what made my Dad the way he was. While he did have a heart of gold, there were two other reasons he served people throughout his life with such conviction.

Number one, I know the horrors he witnessed in the prison camps (death camps), especially the last one, psychologically tortured my Dad as his natural nature was to help people, and he could do nothing to help them. Number two, when you read about the situations Dad found himself in during combat on the battlefield and then in captivity, you would probably come to the same conclusion as me. There is NO logical reason he should have lived, not THAT many times.

I think my Dad knew this more than anyone and spent the rest of his life serving and touching people's lives in a very special way. Not taking anything away from the heroes who died all around my Dad, it just seems like he was spared for a reason. I know my Dad felt he owed a huge debt to God and spent the rest of his life repaying it with true pride and unselfish conviction. As I mentioned previously, Dad really cared about the people of this town and their well-being; as a sergeant in WWII, he felt the same way about his men.

Dad always said, "As long as the guys were bitching, I knew they were alright, but when they got quiet…." The few times I heard this, he usually trailed off right there, but this is when he would worry. I could see it in that stare again. It's like his brain would go on rewind, and he would see flashes of all those times. I imagine these quiet times were just after a hard-fought battle where some of the guys were lost or when they knew they were going into hell just up the road.

4

PIANO STORY

I remember a classic story Dad told me just before he left for the war. The Georgia State Guard put him in charge of all the guns to get the local guys of fighting age trained and familiarized with the weapons they would be using in battle. Being in charge of all the guns, Dad said to me, "Well, I didn't know where I was going to keep these guns, I didn't want to upset Mama, so I decided I'll put 'em in the back of the piano, nobody ever plays it."

Well, it just so happened that after church on this particular Sunday, all the women decided to go over to my grandmother's house for lunch. You already guessed what happened next, didn't you? Of course, wouldn't you know that one of them went over and sat down to, I'm sure, play some church song on the piano? I don't know where Dad was, but he was probably praying no one would decide to play it.

Dad did not know these women were coming over. Dad told me, "I heard Mama call me, Roy, Roy, this piano won't play. Can you see what's wrong with it?"

Oh, I would have loved to have seen Dad have to remove those guns one by one in front of all those women. You can imagine their reactions, and you know that was the talk of the town for years to come.

ROBERT GILBERT

GEORGIA·STATE·GUARD

HONORABLE
·DISCHARGE·
— To —

Roy Alonza Gilbert

Address __Tennille, Georgia__

County __Washington__ Unit No. __209__

IS HEREBY DISCHARGED FROM THE SERVICE OF THE GEORGIA STATE GUARD

Date of entry into Service __April 15, 1942__

Date of Discharge __March 1, 1943__

Rank at time of Discharge __Private First Class__

Reason for Discharge __Entering U. S. Armed Forces__

Character of Soldier __Excellent__

By order of the Commanding Officer:

Adjutant, Georgia State Guard

This, the __12th__ day of __April__ 194__3__

OUR GIFT

WAR STORIES

WORLD WAR II North West Europe (1944-1945)

5

THE RAILROAD

It was a miserable rainy night. Everyone was in full-length rain gear with the hoods of their jackets pulled over their helmets, as it was raining so hard. They were walking along at the base of an elevated railroad track through the countryside. Naturally, it would be suicide to walk at the top of the railroad track, which was 15 to 20 feet up on a clear night, as you would be a sitting duck. However, on this night, you could hardly see your hand in front of your face. As they sloshed through the water, it was getting deeper. My Dad said they stopped and all decided collectively, "The hell with this, we're going up there."

As they walked up the embankment, they suddenly experienced a "twilight zone" moment. As Dad and his men reached the top, they began blending in with people doing the same thing coming up from the other side. Lots of them. Dad knew very quickly they were not American troops. I don't know if he knew from his assignment that no other American troops would be in that particular area or if he heard them speaking German. I wish he was here for me to ask. Anyway, somehow, they all kept their cool and didn't panic, just simply blended in. I don't know how many men were in Dad's platoon at that time, but I remember he said they were far outnumbered. They were walking shoulder to shoulder with the German army. Realize they all looked exactly alike in rain gear. I recall asking Dad, as a kid, "What if one of them had said something to you?"

Dad said, "That would have been all she wrote."

They walked about two miles, which must have been the longest two miles they had ever walked. Can you imagine the heart rate or the feeling in the gut? Somehow, Dad noticed the railroad was curving off to the right up ahead and noticed somewhat of a path going off the embankment veering left. Dad sent the message back very quietly from one man to the next to veer left at the turn. Luckily, they had all stayed on the left side, and no Germans had crossed over to mix in. They all veered off, and some probably became a little more spiritual that night, as not a shot was fired.

Remember, there was no moon, and the rain never stopped pounding, forcing all to keep their heads down and losing peripheral vision to a degree from the rain jacket hood. Thank God no German soldier decided to get chatty that monsoon night with one of our guys. I think all the guardian angels were with them on that night.

6

REBEL

Yep. That name fit him perfectly. Dad said, "Rebel was the best soldier I ever fought alongside with. My number one scout."

Hearing the conviction in my Dad's voice left no doubt about that. Rebel was quite a character. I wish I would have asked Dad more about him. From what I recall, Dad said Rebel could move out across any terrain really fast and be elusive. He always seemed to show up at the right place at the right time, and Dad said, "Boy, he sure hated the enemy!"

He seemed to be somewhat of a natural comedian. What little humor Dad and his guys could find over there usually involved Rebel. Like one incident, Dad had told Rebel many times before, "Rebel, when you light up a cigarette, cup it, they're gonna take your damn head off one night."

The reason is obvious, you will become a perfect target for a sniper. Dad said Rebel's response was, "Yea, Sarge, yea, yea!" and kind of laughed it off. Then Dad would see him soon forget and do it again. Well, one night, they came across an abandoned farm and decided to try to get some much-needed rest or at least chill out for a while. I don't know how Dad and his men ever really rested or slept. This night was no exception.

They were by a barn with a few haystacks around. Just as they were getting settled in, Rebel was sitting at the base of one of those haystacks. Dad saw him fire up a cigarette, no cupping, of course, take a big drag, and as he was lying back on the haystack, BOOM! A sniper bullet just barely grazed his forehead. It's lucky for Rebel he laid back when he did. Dad could see Rebel dive for cover as they all were, so he knew he was okay. Then, out of the silence, Rebel yelled out, "They tried to kill me!!"

Dad yelled back, "Rebel, they've been trying to kill you since you stepped off the damn boat!"

That created a little nervous laughter for the guys and relief that Rebel was okay. Needless to say, Rebel never forgot to "cup" after that. It also appears to me that Rebel was a natural-born killing machine on the battlefield. Dad never said that, but from the bits and pieces I've heard, that's the impression I got. Like, one time, after one of their battles, most of the enemy was taken out, but two Germans were in a pillbox still firing a 50-caliber machine gun at them. Dad said, "Boy, they were giving us hell! So, two of our guys made their way around and managed to throw grenades close to the pillbox. The firing stopped, and when they closed in, they found the two Germans in the pillbox, one dead and one....." at this point, Dad stopped talking, looked away briefly, and then looked back at me, motioning with his hand around his chin and lower jaw, then said, "All this was gone, but he was still alive."

As a fairly young kid, I was getting those visions again on this horrible scene and feeling sorry for the guy. I asked Dad, "What did you all do?" Dad gazed off again, and by the look in his eyes, I wished I had not asked. After a few long seconds, Dad said just one word. "Rebel." I never asked him about that one again because I had a strong feeling Dad was "one of those men" who tossed the grenades. Another time, Dad and Rebel were on a reconnaissance mission and came upon an area where a big, flat rock jutted out from a mountain just across from them. There was a valley between them. Out on that rock ledge walked a German soldier all alone. The guy had no shirt on, and Dad said, "Boy, he had the muscles, really built! Looked like a bodybuilder!"

They watched for a couple of minutes to see if others were going to join him, but they never did. Dad said he just stood there, crossed his arms in front of his chest, and gazed out across the landscape, looking very proud. Well, you can imagine what was going on with Rebel. He was chomping at the bit. Dad knew Rebel could pick him off, so he once again held the reins back and told him no. I'm sure in Dad's mind, he thought, "Why?"

It could open up a pandora's box because they could never see who was with him. Come to think of it, whoever was with the "muscle man" was not stupid enough to make themselves a target like him. I wonder how they knew he was German? Maybe it was because of his pants, boots, or, most likely, because he was wearing his helmet. The only other memories I have of Rebel come later in the book. One incident occurs in the chapter "The Farmhouse – Most Personal Kill." The other is in my Dad's writings, which point out examples of his elusiveness to the enemy and what I refer to as one of those "Twilight Zone" moments my Dad was experiencing, and Rebel was right in the middle of it.

THE PURPLE HEART

The Purple Heart is a medal presented to service members who have been wounded or killed in action as a result of enemy action while serving in the U.S. military. A Purple Heart is a solemn distinction and means a service member has greatly sacrificed themselves, or paid the ultimate price, while in the line of duty.

All I know about this incident is that all hell had broken loose during the heat of battle. Dad was running from one area to another but came upon a row of concertina wires. He ran alongside it, looking for cover and trying to make it to the forest in the distance. The next thing he knew, he woke up being jostled around in the back of a Jeep that was hauling ass. I remember Dad's Georgia slang, "Boy, they were apen it!"

I know, I've never heard that expression anywhere else, either.

OUR GIFT

It's a Georgia expression during that era that translates to "moving very fast!" Dad said when he sat up, the two GIs in the front seat turned around and described their reaction as being startled or surprised. Dad described the look on their faces as if they had just seen a ghost. After a brief pause, one of the GIs said, "We thought you were dead. You came flying over that row of concertina wire like a ragdoll and landed right by us. We just threw you in and kept going as fast as we could."

As they headed to the medic, they told him what had happened. They said, "You hit a landmine when you were running."

Dad took a hit with shrapnel in the back from the landmine. As a kid, I remember asking him what they did at Medic. I can hear his voice now, "Well, they dug one piece out and left another. They sewed me up then - back out."

Again, as a kid, I remember the words "dug a piece out" really creeped me out. I never found out if he was laid up for a while or if he did just go right back out. Knowing my Dad, I'm sure he went back out ASAP. The part about this one that really *"blows my mind"* is that two guys just happened to be speeding along in a Jeep through a hell zone and how at least one of the guys in the Jeep is even able to focus on my Dad with all that was going on around them, from the time he hit the landmine to almost landing in the Jeep.

He literally landed right in front of them, the direction they were going, anyway. What are the odds? Right place at the right time, good luck, or divine intervention? With all this aside, how do you step on a landmine and not get killed, or at least lose a body part, especially when the force of the explosion was strong enough to toss a 190-pound body over that big roll of wire? I'm sure a ballistic expert could have an explanation. Dad could run really fast at that age. Another way to look at it, maybe that landmine saved his life by getting him out of the line of fire, over a row of concertina wire that was a nightmare of a barrier to the safety of the back of a speeding Jeep.

8

WHEN HEAVEN APPEARS IN HELL

One saying that seems to prove itself time after time in combat is "always expect the unexpected." I guess a better saying, or at least a more logical one, is you can never let your guard down. Also, the most brilliant plan from the best tacticians can turn useless in the blink of an eye. Dad and his men were on the edge of a forest just inside the tree line late one day at dusk. As they were moving along somehow, they realized that German soldiers were coming at them from ahead. It gets worse. They are coming from the forest side and from behind. They are trapped. Surrounded! The only way out was across an open field about three-quarters of a mile to the forest on the other side.

There was still enough light to see countless small ditches, and what I recall Dad saying was, "low fences of some kind" to hurdle over to get there. Realizing there were no options, they took off. They didn't get much of a head start when the bullets started whizzing by. They were hurdling over obstacle after obstacle, not reaching halfway, when the mortars started hitting. Dad said, "This was the most scared I ever was in combat."

Remember, it was an open field with nowhere to hide (the ditches were far too shallow), and mortars were raining down. Dad said, "The forest looked far away, impossible to reach. Boy, I didn't think any of us were gonna make it! Just about the time I was thinking that thought, I got tripped up hurdling over one of those damn ditches. I hit hard enough to almost knock the wind out of me. Somehow, as I was starting to lift myself up, I noticed my bible had fallen out of my jacket pocket, and it was lying right in front of my face."

I don't remember how old I was when Dad told me this for the first time, but I do remember that he turned away for a few seconds. I was old enough to realize what was happening. However, in those few seconds, I realized, wow, I think Dad's getting emotional. That never happens. Something must have happened after he fell. He turned back around and said, "It was opened up to the bible verse—*though I walk through the valley of the shadow of death, I will fear no evil: for thou art with me;* and my eyes locked in on that verse."

After a few seconds of my brain processing it all, I said, "How did you see? Wasn't it almost dark?"

Dad said, "Oh yeah, but the sky was lit up from all the artillery. It's like I had a bright light right over me."

I asked, "What did you do then?"

Dad said, "I put the bible back in my pocket and moved out." Knowing my Dad the way I do, when time stood still, though it was just a few seconds, it was long enough for him to focus on that verse. Out of all the verses it could have been, THAT particular verse gave him renewed confidence at a time when he needed it the most. Again, knowing my Dad the way I do, the second half of that run to that forest became easy. With hell still raining down and still hurdling over obstacles, I know his mindset was, "They can't touch me now, at least not this time."

I never found out how many men were lost in that field or if they all made it. I was so amazed at his story I forgot to ask. While many of us think we have faith, it "radiated" from Dad. It's like it was a part of his DNA. I always admired that.

ROBERT GILBERT

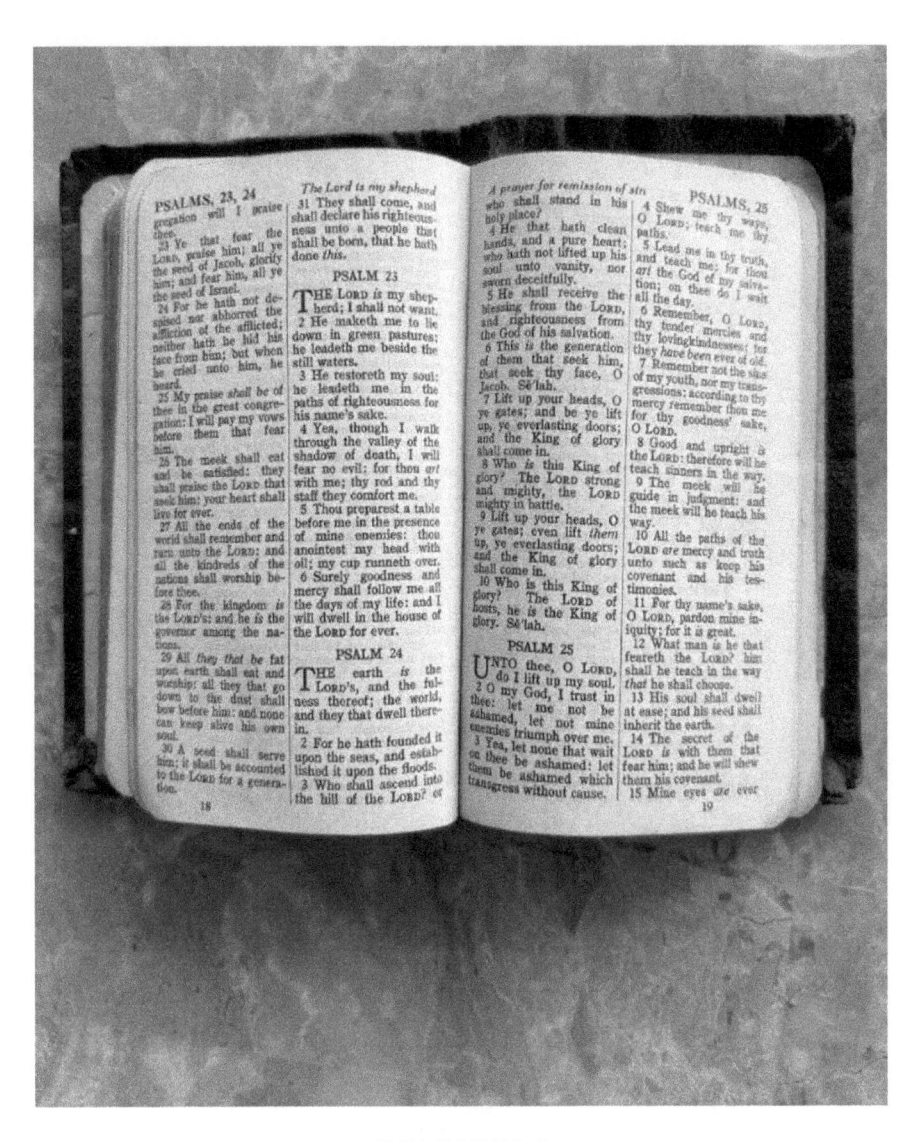

PSALM 23.4

9

TRAGEDY IN THE TRENCHES

This story captures just one of the hellish skirmishes these young soldiers endured during battle.

Their platoon was advancing towards the German border in the Grémecey Forest on this early foggy morning as they crossed an open field to get to the woods. Unexpectedly, the fog lifted exposing them to frontal fire from the Germans. They raced forward and fell into shallow trenches that were left over from WWI as artillery was being fired upon them.

This story was narrated by Dad and written by Mom 60 years after this incident. This narrated version was toned down somewhat from what he described to me as a young boy which will follow this narration.

Dad's narration of this story is written by Mom, as follows:

OUR GIFT

1.

We were in the Grimacy Forrest outside of Nancy France the first part of Dec. '44 — It was cold but no snow. It was early morning & we were advancing. My platoon was in the lead, heading for the German border. We had not yet reached the Siegfried Line. We came upon an open field we had to cross to get to another section of trees. We were in heavy fog so felt fairly safe. Just as we reached the edge of the woods the fog magically lifted and at the same time we received frontal fire from the Germans. We raced forward and fell into a trench left from WWI — it wasn't deep, but enough so that it gave us some cover. We continued being fired upon, but in small amounts.

The four of us were sitting in a circle & I could hear our artillery coming in — I had a feeling they were firing short by the sound of it. The boy next to me said something about his 3 children & I said you look too young to have 3 children & he handed me his wallet.

ROBERT GILBERT

2 with pictures of his family. One shell came in right where we were sitting, killing that boy & wounding another. I placed his wallet in his shirt. The reason the shell didn't kill us all is because in the last war when it was dug, it must have been 15 or 20 ft. deep, and had filled in with leaves & such over the years which made it very soft. The other boy and I got very very lucky that day. About that time the rest of the company came into the woods, and the enemies began to retreat.

OUR GIFT

As Dad Described it to Me: Dad and two of his men were sitting in what was described to me as a trench that through the years had filled partially up with layers of mulch. One guy sat directly across from Dad and if they both stretched out their legs their feet would almost touch. This gives you an idea of how close they were sitting together. The other guy sat to my dad's left. I imagine they were quite comfortable with nature's cushion layer beneath them. They must have been somewhat relaxed as the guy across from Dad said, "Look what I have to look forward to when we get out of here.", tossing Dad the wallet. Dad opened up his wallet and saw a picture of a girl and three children. Just at that moment their rare, peaceful time ended with the horrifying whistling sound of "incoming." Dad said he drew his legs in against his body and tucked his head against his knees in the fetal position and he told me, "It sounded like it was right on top of us." It was. The missile hit right between Dad and the guy across from him. Dad said it did not go off until it hit the rock bed deep below the thick mulch layer quite a few feet down. The projection of course went straight back up. When Dad's senses came back and he could focus, the guy to his left was gone, thrown out of the trench and wounded, and the guy in front was still sitting up with his back against the wall of the trench. Dad noticed it was only his top half. The first time I heard that story as a young kid, my mouth was probably hanging open and as my mind cleared of that horrible scene and I could breathe again I asked him only what a kid would, "What did you do with his wallet?" I remembered the look in Dad's eyes at certain times when he would tell me these stories. I learned as I got older what those few seconds of a stare-into-nowhere were all about. After a few seconds of just that, Dad said, "Well, I just put it back in his pocket to help with his ID." Dad did not have a scratch or even suffer hearing loss from that one. – AMAZING.

I also learned later that this artillery was from friendly fire that caused this. Of course, our "friendly fire" intentions were to fire artillery over Dad and his guys hitting the enemy ahead in the forest and softening them up. The coordinates got screwed up as Dad said he thought they were firing short in his narration to Mom. Sad, but this happened a lot during that era. Things have improved with pinpoint accuracy and technology.

10

TWO VERSIONS OF DAD

As a kid somewhere south of puberty I took one of many rides downtown with my dad to the drugstore after hours at night, to get medication for someone in need. The customer met us there and I stayed in the car. Although I knew how Dad's relationship was with the public, I noticed that particular night the interaction on the sidewalk in front of the store between them. As a kid, I thought wow, they are so thankful and I always noticed how much more relaxed they appeared when they left as opposed to when they had arrived. They were just so relieved to be getting the help they needed for themselves or a family member. As I have said before, they knew that he really cared and they all showed true gratitude. Just as I was observing how nice and reassuring Dad was to this person, that everything was going to be OK, and thinking how many he has done the same thing for and how they all seem to love him an out-of-left field thought popped into my head. I thought about Dad going into battle and actually having to KILL others in order to survive. Being such a contrast of scenes from what I was witnessing at this moment was really weird and difficult to even think about. I suddenly realized there were two versions of my dad. I think what "triggered" that thought was, that I had become aware that when Dad would make those runs at night, he carried a concealed Smith & Wesson 357 magnum. He always wore a white t-shirt with a leather shoulder holster on his left side. He would cover that with an unbuttoned white or tan pharmacy jacket for quick access. No one could ever guess he was packing. On the way home that night I asked him what it was like in war to have to kill somebody. He paused and said, "Well, Rob, the first time that happened, I felt like the entire German Army was coming after me, but then…" That's where my dad left off but I knew exactly where he was coming from even back then. I've never been in combat, thank God, but I'm sure in the "fury" of combat a person would not have time to think or they would die. I can only imagine that most young men sent into battle for the first time feel the same way my dad did. Think of yourself in that position. You look down the barrel of your gun, line your sight up on a person around your age, pull the trigger, and watch them drop. Even though you know they would have done the same to you, it has to be a sickening feeling if you are a normal person with a conscious. I'm sure that sickening feeling doesn't last long when the bullets are flying at you and you see your friends dropping. I'm sure after the first kill, a person in "survival mode" would go on "autopilot", as there really is no choice if you are going to live. Realize that not one man who went to fight WWII questions "why" they were there. They had the support of the entire USA behind them and the cause. They were not fighting just to save their country but on a more personal level their very own families. This was the battle of good versus evil which I'm sure made a difference in the minds of these boys having to kill for the first time. A few days after our conversation it got my young mind to thinking, killing the enemy at a distance is one thing, but what about up close and personal? I had to know so I caught him at the perfect time. After he had just finished some intense yard work, he was taking a water break under the shade of the trees in the backyard. I knew he would be "chilled out" enough for me to ask this question. When I did, he just kind of stared at me for a few long seconds which at first made me wonder if I should have asked. I think at that moment he was wondering maybe if I was too young for this one but he knew I needed to know. I was relieved for the silence to be broken with, "Well Rob," and boy was I in for a ride.

The following story combines Dad's exact words from a recording and my memory of this encounter I heard many times throughout the years.

11

THE FARMHOUSE AND MOST PERSONAL KILL

Dad said, "It was sometime in August of '44 we were strung out on an attack route. What our objective was, I'll never know, I don't remember. My squad was in the lead at this time. We had a point man out and were fixin' to put out a man on the right flank. We called in the one that had been out there." Dad said Rebel walked up and said, "What ya' lookin' at, Sarge?" Dad said, "I'm not sure. I think I saw a faint puff of smoke up ahead." Now, from what I gathered from Dad, Rebel was always "jacked up" and it makes sense that Rebel volunteered to go and take the guy's place that came back in, especially after dad told him what he thought he saw. That's when Dad said, "I'll go with you." I think Dad's intuition was on target and he didn't want Rebel to be alone. So, Dad and Rebel went out on the right flank. Dad said, "Rebel and I were rather fast walkers and we walked quite a way and didn't realize it but got ahead of the column. We came into an apple orchard and I saw a barn up ahead." Rebel said, "Well, they've been here and it hadn't been long because this is where they climbed out of this hole." Behind the barn was a farmhouse surrounded by forest. Dad told me it was kind of secluded. They briefly checked out the scene and noticed a guard in the barn. Behind the barn and just to the left was the farmhouse where roughly ten to twelve Germans were in the room. Some were sitting around a table eating while others were just standing around. Dad said, "It appeared they were having a meeting of some sort by their mannerisms." Dad and Rebel already had their plan of attack but had to get past the guard. Well, next the unexpected happened right in front of them. The guard still in the barn walked over, and straddled a log, setting his mess kit down on the log and his Burp Gun (machine gun) on a box right next to him. They were lucky the guard got hungry at this time and felt secure enough in this secluded location to UNBELIEVABLY have his back turned to the open barn door! Now it's go-time. Dad's words were, "I got to the barn and as I went to the open door, this kraut was sitting there eating out of a mess kit. He had his back to me and I told him to put his hands over his head in German. So, he looked around, we made eye contact for a couple of seconds and I'll never forget his smile. He smiled and then reached for his Burp Gun. So, I fired, shot him in the back." Now, you can imagine what happened after Dad fired that first shot alerting the Germans in the farmhouse. Well, actually, you can't. They had to have moved at lightning speed through the barn to take a position in front of the farmhouse to pull off what came next. Remember, they had this plan for this moment. Dad realized the walls of the farmhouse were stone, which the bullets would ricochet off of. Dad said, "I stood to the left and Rebel to the right. I shot through the right window and Rebel shot through the left window in a cross-fire pattern." I remember the first time I heard that as a kid thinking wow, it's like a tornado of bullets ricocheting off the walls like that or a blender. Dad said, "We began to fire, I mean we fired until both clips were gone out of our rifles and so we reloaded and fired again." We pulled the trigger and popped in clips faster than we ever had. About the time they were finishing up, the rest of the platoon arrived, and Dad said a guy yelled, "Where the hell did ya'll get machine guns?" They all stood there with all guns aiming at the farmhouse. Dad said there was an eerie silence, then the door popped open. Out walked an unarmed German officer (Lieutenant) without a scratch on him. Dad's men swarmed the farmhouse and came back pretty quickly. They told Dad "They're all dead and they put him in a safe-room." Dad said, "As I was asking the officer in German to put his hands up, he just kept glaring and staring at me. The officer finally blurted something out in German, so Dad asked his guy, Schwartz, who knew the language, "What the hell did he say?" Schwartz said, "He said he will only surrender to an officer of at least his rank." You see, my dad, being a sergeant was beneath him in his eyes. Dad did say he looked down his nose at me the whole time. Well, you can imagine how Rebel was reacting. Rebel really loved my dad and could not handle him being talked down to like that so he was naturally ready to take the officer out. Rebel was saying something like, "I'll kill him, I'll kill him right here, Sarge!" Dad told me, "I just looked at Rebel and said 'No'." It was at this point the German Lieutenant started speaking English. He knew it all along! I think when he saw Rebel wanting to kill him, he softened up." Now that Dad knew he could understand and speak English, he asked him again, "Put your hands up! Nope, he wasn't going to do it." The officer said, "Well, get me an officer and I'll surrender." So, I said 'No, put your hands up, there is no officer here!" Again, the officer said, "No!" This time rather defiantly. I guess by this time he realized Dad wasn't going to let Rebel kill him. Dad said, "Then all of a sudden, around the corner came Lieutenant Thomas. He came around from the back side of the house and he said, 'Now, put your hands up. I'm an officer and I'll take your surrender.', then there was a pause on the tape…" Rebel and I did not go in the room, the other soldiers checked it out for us. We never talked about it…we just went on to where the crossroad was."

My Afterthoughts:

My question to Dad now regarding the German guard in the barn would be, "What if he did surrender, what would you have done with him, especially with a farmhouse full of Germans just feet ahead?" Knowing my dad, the way I do, I really do know the answer. My dad knew he would never surrender all along, but he just couldn't bring himself to shoot the guy in the back at that close of range without giving him a chance. Not to take anything away from the infamous Rebel, but he would not have wasted time talking. I wish I had thought to ask Dad if he ever considered waiting for the rest of the platoon to catch up before making the attack. I'm sure Dad and Rebel had their reason. I specifically remember Dad's words to Schwartz to interpret. I can hear it now, plain as day. With dad's heavy, rolling Georgia accent, (gotta say it fast) It sounded like "Whatdahelldesay?", which translates to, "What the hell did he say?" I remember this one quite a few times over the years. I liked to hear him say that. You know it's amazing how writing these stories affects me now. I mean, I put myself in his position in my early twenties. He was just a kid! He had just experienced a personal kill, that's bad enough. Immediately after that was the farmhouse. There is no sugar-coating the farmhouse incident. As ugly as this may sound, it was a total slaughter. I don't care how "battle-hardened" Dad and Rebel had become at this point, this one got to both of them. The fact they never discussed it again speaks volumes. Just think of all the things that could have gone wrong but didn't. It's not like they had a practice run for THIS kind of an attack, it went PERFECT. From a tactician's point of view, I know the element of surprise is everything and probably would be viewed as a brilliant plan but Dad and Rebel were the last ones that would have thought that. The times Dad told me this one over the years he never boasted about it. I guess you could say he came across to me more monotone and matter-of-fact. I asked Dad a question a kid would ask. "Did you ever go in that farmhouse?" He had that distant stare into nowhere again, slowly shook his head, and said, "No." Even though I discussed details of that incident with Dad over the years, I never asked him about going in the farmhouse again, obviously because I already knew. The feeling I got years ago by the look on his face and that stare into nowhere was, that I think he saw more than he wanted to see, even if it was just a glimpse. The combination of the "tone" of his voice at the end of that recording and me flashing back to the look on his face when he told me about not going in that farmhouse years ago was weird. When Dad said Rebel and I did not go in the room, the other soldiers checked it out for us, we never talked about it, we just went on to where the crossroad was. It gave me the same feeling I felt back then, feeling what Dad felt. I know I have referred to Rebel as a killing machine on the battlefield but I know this man had a human side also. My dad would have never thought as highly of him if he did not. Just the fact Rebel never brought this incident up again to my dad speaks for itself. Dad said, "We never talked about it". They were on the same page that day emotionally. I would guess numb and somewhat sad but they knew they did what they had to do. I'm sure after the adrenaline wore off, on that long walk to the crossroad, Dad and Rebel reflected back and realized they were not alone back at the farmhouse as it simply went too smooth and easy. They knew they were not just lucky, but were truly blessed. In the big picture, this is merely one small "blip" on the radar of "good versus evil" that when added up eventually won that war for us.

OUR GIFT

12

THE CAPTURE AND INTERROGATION

The next story is of Dad's capture and interrogation by the SS. Mom wrote every word in detail as Dad narrated. Over the years Mom's handwriting has faded so you will find a typed transcription of her written words.

I found this FASCINATING, to say the least for many reasons. With the amount of detail that Dad gives in the upcoming chapters, it pulls you in and it makes you feel like you are walking in his shoes. Those details also help us get a visual picture of the scene and in turn, give us a very clear idea of not what just the body goes through physically but psychologically. The nervous system is tested to the maximum by going through this hell. As you put yourself in his place, you will see what I mean. Get ready for the emotional roller coaster the next few chapters will take you on.

Writing Transcribed:

It all began in WWII when I was taken prisoner of war by the Germans near Bitche in Dec. 1944. I remember the rocks, large rocks the size of a refrigerator or a stove. We had moved into this area, about 14 of us, the night of Dec. 15, 1944.

In the afternoon of that day, we were pretty well dug in below the rocks. I was in a machine gun emplacement. A recon vehicle drew up, which was a reconnaissance outfit, that was coming back from an area a little ahead of us. We asked them what was on the hill in front of us, and the reply was, "10,000 Kraut Eaters!" They then added something more traumatic than 10,000 Germans. They said, "The SOB's shot down Glen Miller's plane!" The plane that was bringing him from England to Paris. Miller, of course, was the leader of the 8th Air Force Band, and his music was loved by all the GI's, in fact, it was THE music of WWII.

Back to the Rocks; Dec. 16, 1944, our objective was the town of "Bitche." This town was in Alsace Lorraine which was very near the border of Germany. The rocks were on top of the hill which was flat for several hundred yards, and we could see that when it dropped off, the forest began.

Just before we moved out, we saw three Germans coming towards us. They had no idea we were there. As they came closer, we could see that one was an officer flanked by two non-coms. We shot the non-coms and motioned for the officer to come to us. He was "SS", and as cool as he could be. He had no problem speaking English and said that we must have bypassed his men who were behind us. He was so convincing in telling his story, that we assumed that K Co. (which was on our right flank) had engaged his men, which of course was not true.

I don't remember what we did with the SS officer, but soon after we shoved off, one of our men, Mike Hayes, had been sick all night and we agreed he should stay behind in the rocks.

Combat Platoon strength is 36 men, we only had 14. Replacements were coming and going out so fast, that I could not remember their names. Five of us had been together since we were at St. Lo; Mike, Rebel, Schwartz, Hendrick, and myself.

We shoved off across the field towards the woods. Just as we got there, we heard machine gunfire behind us. I glanced back and saw the men on the ground. Whether they were hit by the cross-

OUR GIFT

fire, or whether they "hit the ground," I will never know.

We four were in the woods now. I realized that I had forgotten much after 51 years, but this day I remember well. I can see this scene as plainly as I did when it happened.

I looked to my right just after we entered the woods. I saw 3 Germans about 200 ft. from us, they were looking off in the other direction and their backs were towards us. Just as I raised my rifle, Hendricks said, "Gilbert, drop your gun." This I did. We had been too long together so there was no "why?" Directly ahead of us about 75 ft. was a German on the ground behind a machine gun and another crouched beside him with a pistol in his hand motioning for us to come forward. This all happened in a matter of seconds. Now if I had fired at one of the three, would the one on the machine gun have waited for me to shoot one of his own men before cutting us down? Hendrick was about 3 ft. behind me and slightly to the right, and Schwartz was on my left. Rebel, I didn't see at all. The crouched German yelled "surrender" and we stepped forward just as the man behind the machine gun made a move, I thought to shoot. I was so scared that I did not think of the classic surrender method which was to knock your helmet off and place your hands behind your head. The German shouted again, "*Hande hinter deinem Kopf!*" (place your hands behind your head). We had all shouted this to the Germans many times. This we did.

The crouched soldier got up, and with pistol in hand, took us to a Chateau, which was not far, but deeper in the woods. The soldier behind the machine gun stayed where he was. It was at this time we noticed that Rebel was not with us.

We three were held in the yard of the Chateau. Shortly, an officer and seven soldiers came out. The officer told us to put all we had on the ground. I had my gas mask pouch (no gas mask) that held my chocolates, cigarettes, and other things like 30-

caliber ammunition.

I remember that he asked us if we knew who had us. I answered, "Yes, the SS." He then asked what we did with "SS" when we captured them. I told him that we took them out of the line of fire and to the rear. "You don't shoot them?", he asked. I said no to this. Not knowing what he knew or what he heard, made my mouth even drier. He then said, "Do you expect this?", as he drew his finger across his throat. I told him that I did not and that we expected to be treated according to the rules of the "Geneva Conference." He said, "You are quite right, we are not barbaric, you are the barbarians."

Each of us had our belongings on the ground in front of us. The officer approached me, said something in German, and the next thing I knew I was on the ground. Whether he hit or pushed me I don't know. For the first time, Schwartz spoke and said, "Gilbert he wants your bible." I had my Gideon Testament in my shirt pocket and had not put it on the ground. I took it out and gave it to him. He looked at it, thumbed through it, and started to hand it back. Then he pulled it back and did the same thing again. I have the Testament today. Now, up to this point I remember very clearly each event in sequence as it happened, but now I remember events, but not the length of time in between.

In the yard I thought about several things. We did not talk to each other. I am sure that Schwartz and Hendrick were wondering as I was, where "Rebel" could be. I was also wondering if our Company was going to attack the woods. I knew if they did, they would hit it with artillery first. I wanted out of there!

I realized that there was something going on between the Germans. They seemed to be arguing. Schwartz was picking this up and I would not know until later what this conversation was all about.

OUR GIFT

I remember next, the three of us were in an upstairs room of a house. This was probably the first night. We were given a very thick and meaty soup, it was good. We were hungry and by now we thought that maybe they were not going to kill us. The guard who brought it to us was proud of the soup. "Good swine flesh", he said, pointing out the hog meat.

Interrogation came later in the night. I remember a nut playing a concertina in the hall and the interrogation room. We were taken in one at a time. The others stayed in the upstairs room.

I was seated at a desk. Behind the desk was the same officer that was with us in the yard. He said that he was going to ask some questions, and that I would answer them or that they had ways to make me talk. All the while the idiot in the hall kept playing the concertina.

The officer began talking about Macon, Georgia and the Dempsey Hotel. I have no idea why or how he knew that I was from that area of Georgia. I don't remember what he asked me, but I do know that I didn't have the slightest idea about the information he wanted. I kept giving my name, rank, and serial number. "Ways" to make me talk were never carried out.

Each of us were taken separately to the interrogation room and asked the same questions. The "threats" were never used on any of us.

The second day we were taken to a large cave filled with civilians where we spent the night. We stood most of the night with our hands against the walls by order of the guards. Throughout the night, small children would come up to us and give us light swats on our legs. These people were from a nearby town, and were in the cave to escape the bombing.

The next day we were marched under guard and placed in the

center of a large factory yard. The buildings were arranged in a quadrangle. On three sides was the factory and the fourth side was open with a road leading in. We three slept in the center with guards nearby. Just as day was breaking we saw a strange sight on the road coming toward us. As the scene got closer, we couldn't believe our eyes. It was a German guard, and "Rebel" pushing a baby carriage! The carriage held a field radio which belonged to the soldier. He placed Rebel with us and joined the guards who were across the way.

At this time Rebel filled us in on many things we did not know about when we were being captured. We learned what all the controversy was among the Germans as we were being captured.

Here is Rebel's story:

As he entered the woods, he could not see the three of us, he was probably not yet in the woods when the firing in the field occurred. He surprised a German soldier and shot him, as he said, "right in the head". He then jumped in a nearby hole and stayed there for a period of time, long enough that the Germans didn't see him, so he was not captured with us. Schwartz (who spoke German) said the argument at the Chateau was about the dead German. Some of the soldiers thought we had shot him, yet the one who brought us in held fast to the fact that we had not fired a shot. He won the argument. They never knew that Rebel was the one who shot him. We never saw the remainder of our company or knew what happened to them.

13

TWILIGHT ZONE MOMENTS

There are several *'Twilight Zone Moments'* for me throughout this book as I am recalling the stories my Dad told me. As you are being taken to the interrogation room, just imagine what thoughts are racing through your head. Now combine that nervous, scared, sickening mindset with the inescapable sound of the concertina before and during interrogation. Weird and creepy. I believe that scene creates a Twilight Zone moment. There were classic comments Dad made about the guy playing the concertina that made me laugh.

How about the scene on the third day of captivity while in the factory yard at daybreak with what they witnessed? Rebel came in with a German guard pushing a baby carriage that held the guard's field radio. That's one strange twilight zone of a scene to start the day with, as well as relief.

14

DAD'S MIRACLE BIBLE

I found the incident in the courtyard of the chateau after Dad was knocked down and Schwartz informed him that they wanted his bible *fascinating*, to say the least. The SS officer took it, thumbed through it, and went to hand it back to Dad. Dad slowly reached out for it, and the SS officer drew it back and thumbed through it again. At this point, most would think he may tear it in half, spit on it, stomp it, and burn it, but NO. The unthinkable happened. He gave it back!! Can you guess what the mindset of the SS officer was at that time? Who knows, but I would guess at that exact moment, the SS officer felt an emotion that was killed off, buried, or erased a long time ago and it woke up a little.

A little voice from deep down in the subconscious that instinctively knows right from wrong. Maybe in his mind, it was a bad omen to destroy or not give it back, or possibly it was a fear. A fear that, by pure gut instinct, tells you that there is something much more powerful than you and to leave it alone. Okay. At this moment, just as I wrote that last line, something really strange happened. I looked up at this bible sitting on the shelf along with Dad's pictures, medals, flag, etc., and just as my eyes were focusing on it, today's first rumbling thunder hit. If it had been thundering, I would have thought nothing of it, but it was the first of that day on 7/13/2023. Well, that got my attention. I got the little bible that went through hell to see what kind of shape it was in. It's definitely well-worn, and the jacket has been detached for as long as I can remember, but it's all still there.

As I thumbed through it, I thought about the SS officer doing the same thing. Weird. Just the thought of the Bible being with Dad every step of the way and what it went through and stayed intact is a miracle. *This Bible* belongs in a museum.

The following day, I was thinking about my incident with the bible, and just for the record, I can understand how some could think I was being dramatic with the timing of the thunder yesterday. Well, number one, I can't lie. Number two, it would not only be corny but in bad taste to make up something like that. Here is a play-by-play on it. The house was totally quiet, except for a floor fan in the other room. Just as I finished the *more powerful than you* line, my brain was screaming, the little bible, it better still be there, I haven't looked in a while! Just as I looked up a millisecond later and caught sight of it being partially blocked by a card, and my eyes focused on it alone, the thunder hit. I have not heard it rumble like that for a while.

It had about a 5-10 second hang time and shook the windows in this old house. My immediate thought was, "Okay! I hear you!" As I said, it really got my attention. It kind of felt like a wake-up call to get the book done. Well, it is done for the most part. Everything that I am capable of writing about is done.

For some reason, on 7/13/23, I could not stop thinking about that incident, so on the spur of the moment, I wrote about it. What are the odds of me even writing about the incident on *that day?* What are the odds of writing *that* particular line, my eyes focusing on the bible and, at *that* exact moment, the thunder hitting for the first time? Anyway, I had no idea how that incident affected me until my daughter called a few minutes after it happened, and I tried to explain it. I could not at first as I got choked up. Yes, I guess it did hit me pretty damn hard. THAT little bible is very special.

ROBERT GILBERT

15

CHRISTMAS EVE THROUGH THE EYES OF A POW

Typed by Staff Sergeant Roy Gilbert

ROBERT GILBERT

Christmas Through the Eyes Of A POW

There were several hundred of us and we had been walking most of the night before and all of the day. Three of us were soldiers of the 35th Division 320 Infantry-Third Army; Hendricks, Schwartz and me. All of the others, to the best of my knowledge, were from other outfits. All taken at or near Bastogne. Three of these men later became very close to me. George Rohbock, Jack Hargate and John McGinnis. Rebel (Delmar Stafford) my number one scout, who was captured with me, had been left for dead earlier. Rebel was one of the best soldiers I ever knew. We all had been combat soldiers. We now were all P.O.W.'s,

We were only nine days in captivity and really could not realize that we were prisoners. It took only a few more days for the S.S. (Schutz Staffel) to make believers of us. Most of the nine days were spent on forced march to further us from the other advancing force. These had been long days and nights. I believe that the last shelter was five days earlier at Stalag VB.

The first few days most of the talk was of escape. By this time I believe that we all knew that it was not going to happen. I and my three men tried on the second day of capture to escape. We had only one chance, it just did not work out.

There has been no food except for one loaf

of black German bread for eight men to divide every twenty four hours. For water, if you wanted it, there was snow. Not the same snow that I remembered as a child. There was no joy or excitement in seeing it fall. Some of us already had frozen feet. Snow fell and we hardly saw it, we were so cold…

We had been stripped of our over coats, rain coats, jackets and over boots. We were left with our O.D. shirt and trousers and boots. Some had wool knit caps. I had a cotton undershirt with long sleeves under my shirt. I had a wool knit cap. The cotton undershirt probably kept me from freezing to death. Men did freeze and were left on the road. You walked or you died, just that simple. Warm stalags with libraries and food that was talked about during interrogation was never to come. "Just answer a few questions and you will be on your way by train to such a place…" We told them nothing. Threats of "ways to make you talk" were never carried out.

Someone said we were to cover 30k (18 miles)each day. We could hear guns firing at the ends of the columns. This turned out to be the S.S. killing squad taking care of those who had fallen or could not stay with the main body. The S.S. were masters of moving prisoners. It was unbelievable. I have never seen a more brutal, barbaric, sadistic bunch of people.

These S.S. soldiers were trained from their youth. They were told that they were the greatest and wore handsome uniforms. Any other nationality deserved to die. It was so easy for them to kill.

It was nearly night-fall, sub-zero temperatures and still snowing. We were headed into a state farm. The caretakers of this farm were slave laborers, Czech's and Pole's.

The S.S. for some reason decided to put us up in a very large barn. They could secure us better and at the same time they could rotate in and out of the house nearby. Horses and sheep were put into another area. Once in the barn we fell exhausted onto the ground. The ground was wet with urine from the animals, very cold. We laid very close together in three's, rotating the inside man to the outside every so often.

We could hear talking on the outside. Schwartz, who spoke German, said that the laborers were asking the guards if they could give us food. Sometime later we were brought buckets of grain bran mix. This bran mix was there to feed the pigs. I will never know how nor why, but when I was captured I had been able to keep my steel helmet, not the liner but just the helmet. The helmet was used many times. Later, at one time we were put in railroad cars, sixty and seventy to a car. We used this helmet to urinate in and then it could be poured through the bottom of the car.

The laborers were not allowed to come into the barn so they poured the mix through two slats in the barn door. Those who had mess cups used them and then my helmet was filled. Several of us drank from the helmet. Those poor mistreated laborers had so much compassion for us. From that day till now I have never had a better tasting soup.

We felt better after eating or drinking the mix. It was then that the most wonderful thing happened that I have ever experienced. I will know to my dying day that God looked down on this wretched group and said "These are my boys, they are not perfect in my sight but their cause is just. I will do something nice for them."

Directly across from where we laid was a hay loft and several of the boys crawled into this loft. We laid still, our stomachs filled with the bran. Our backs had warmed the urine under us. There was an unusual quiet in the barn.

Then we heard it...singing. We looked across the way into the loft and saw this soldier standing. He was a very small frail man. He sang "The Lord's Prayer" and then a song named "Jerusalem". I did not remember the name of the second song, George told this to me a few years back. There was not a sound from the P.O.W.'s, the laborers nor the S.S. men. They stared into space. I am sure that each was back to another time and another place most unlike this one.

The soldier finished singing. Some men cursed, some prayed, some cried.

In the forty nine years since, I have never experienced a Christmas program that would ever come close to what God, through this man, did for me and so many others on that night.

I don't know and never will know who this boy was. I do know that he was at the right place at the right time...God bless him.

We slept close together that night rotating the outside man to the inside often.

Too soon we heard the old: "Raus Mit Du." Early on we had learned the hard way its meaning: Move it and move it fast!"

The night was December 24, 1944.

This was only one Christmas for us. Many of us had forty nine others. This was the last for so many who were with us that night.

God Bless the Vietnam boys who spent five, six or seven Christmas's much worse than this.

NAME: Roy A. Gilbert

RANK: Sergeant

OUR GIFT

16

DEATH MARCH TO SANDBOSTEL, GERMANY

While quite short, the following story is incredibly impactful and was typed by Dad. Dad goes back to when he was captured, then the journey to Stalag 11B. They were transported by rail cars (cattle cars) packed in like sardines on forced marches through several of these hell camps. The last march was about 150 miles to Sandbostel. It was the worst march for them. Dad was told they lost over 400 men on that march. My Dad came very close to being one of them. This is his story, in his words, of those four months as a POW.

I was captured Dec. 16, 1944 in Alsace Lorraine. I was now a prisoner of the SS. They were very proud to be members of this unit. They asked me if I was aware of who captured me. I told them I was. They asked me if I expected to be killed and I said no. They said, "You are quite right, we are not Barbarians." I learned later that this was the understatement of the century.

From this point of capture I was placed with several other prisoners and marched to Stalag X11F. I was there for a very short time, I do not remember how long.

We were then marched to Stalag VB at Villengen. Here we were separated into groups, noncommissioned officers in one group and privates in another. After a very short time, we started out and finally arrived at Stalag 11B at Hammerstein. I never saw the privates again.

Stalag 11B was several hundred miles north of VB. Mostly forced march and sometimes in cattle cars, and with only a three inch of sawdust bread daily. We lost a large number of men on this journey.

It was at Stalag 11B that four men decided that if they were going to survive this ordeal that they would have to stick together. This was when George Rohbock, Jack Hargate, John McGinnis and I formed what John called a "Click". We stayed with each other on marches and in cattle cars. When able to sleep we lay close together, rotating the inside man to the outside so that all could have a little warmth. All of our outer garments and overboots had been taken from us. We were never out of the snow.

The forced march from 11B to Sandbostel was our worst. We were literally starving to death. One loaf of black bread each day for seven men. I believe this march was nine or ten days. John was so sick that he could not carry his half blanket so we helped him. My diarrhea was worse. George collapsed in the snow bank. We helped him up. About half way on the march, with blood running out of my shoes, I decided to "cash it in". The SS always moved us. They were masters at moving prisoners. They had a killing squad at the rear of the column and if one soldier fell back that far they were shot. The SS rode motorcycles and bicycles. As I said, I didn't think I was going to make it the rest of the way. We were too close to the killing squad. I dropped to the ground, and as I did George knelt down beside me. He pulled my wool cap from my head and prayed "God help me get this man on his feet". At this time I felt these hard licks on my back and neck. I was being beaten with a rifle butt. I supposed this guard figured, why waste ammunition on this one. God heard George's prayer and he got me up. GEORGE ROHBOCK SAVED MY LIFE. Jack and John were told if they looked back at this that they would be shot. Some way, some how we made it to Sandbostel. Someone, I don't know who, said that we lost over 400 men on this march.

As well as I remember, it was latter days of Feb. 1945 that we arrived at Sandbostel. This camp was guarded by SS and regular soldiers. We did not encounter as much brutality here, and in addition to the bread we got about a pint of grass soup at noon. This soup had a piece rutabaga in it and always maggots, and covered with some kind of mold.

We received one Red Cross parcel here, but at no time did we see a representative from the International Red Cross. I truly believe that this camps' listing had been changed from POW to Internment Camp. Therefore the Red Cross had no reason to come to such camps.

We had to go each day to the French compound to get the soup. This was when we passed a very large compound which held men, women and children who all looked like death. They were all dressed in striped clothing and all marked with the Star of David. I did not at this time know anything about the Holocaust, and apparently no one else did. These people were fed out of troughs just as live-stock are fed. We passed the compound each day. Dead people were all over the place but nobody seemed to care.

Things went on about the same until a few days before liberation. We could hear artillery fire in the distance and felt that freedom might be close. We also noticed that there were many more SS there than usual. We were not allowed out of our compound. We heard constant machine gun fire for two or three days and nights. The machine guns stopped and we were told that we could go to the kitchen. The main street leading to the kitchen was laden with dead bodies of the Jewish people.

Liberation came the next day which was April 30, 1945. The British soldiers said that the SS had literally burned up the tower guns killing these people. The smell was so bad that the British soldiers had to go get their gas masks and come back in.

As we departed this place there were large piles of bodies everywhere. The British had brought in civilians from the nearby towns to gather and pile the bodies. After fifty two years, this is what I remember.

INTERESTING SIDE NOTE:

After my dad's beating on the march, when they arrived at Sand bostel, an interesting interaction took place between my Dad and one of the German guards that night. As the men lay exhausted, trying to bed down, a guard (not SS) came over and stood close to Dad. Communication was non-existent between guards and prisoners, as you can imagine. Dad said this guard just kind of looked off to not make it obvious and to my dad's surprise spoke English to him. He quietly said, "I have never seen a human being beaten so severely, and live." That was all that was said. The way Dad described the guard's tone and referred to Dad as a "human being" makes me realize this guard had empathy. Just the fact that he took time to speak those words, speaks volumes.

ROBERT GILBERT

17

THE INTERVIEW 1992

Well, the surprises keep coming. I am at this point done with the book since I wrote about the miracle bible. Just by pure chance, I came across the following story transcribed by Gene V. Sorensen from a taped interview with my Dad back in 1992. Gene and George Rohbuck attended the same church. George Rohbuck, you remember, was the one who saved Dad's life and introduced these two. While in the previous chapters, you have already read most of what is in the following interview, they each contain information that the other does not.

In Dad's writings, he goes into more detail about the interrogation with the SS, the bible incident, and Rebel. I think Dad felt some things were too personal to talk about. However, the interview contained information about where Dad took basic training, the route he took to Europe, and after fighting in the hedgerows on the edge of Saint-Lo, France, what other larger towns they hit after that. He also tells where he was taken after capture, as well as the dates of these occurrences. I always thought it would have been awesome to map his path, and "The Interview" more than makes up for that.

Another *great* find! I was *clueless* about this interview and *only* found it because it was meant to be. I am convinced of that and sure it was not just by chance, as the circumstances leading up to the find were just too weird. Until I read this interview, I never knew Dad was as bad off, near death, as he was at Sandbostel. He never told us. At the end of the interview, just before liberation, they were all at their worst point health-wise, and I believe George did not think my Dad was going to make it. The line George threw at Dad at this low point, maybe out of pure desperation, I feel like he was trying to bring out what little fight Dad had left in him, if any. I will *never* forget that line. No need for me to write it here. It's the last line in the interview. Very impactful.

The only two personal possessions Staff Sergeant Roy Gilbert carried with him from enlistment, throughout all the battles, his capture and captivity were his Gideon Bible and masonic ring. You will notice these items are mentioned on the first page of the interview. We still have these items today.

ROBERT GILBERT

Interview – Transcribed

This interview was transcribed by Gene V. Sorensen from a taped interview with some additions from a personal conversation with Roy Gilbert.

```
Two American Prisoners of War During WWII

The following is a story of two American
soldiers during the dark days of WWII in Europe.
T/Sgt. Roy Gilbert from Georgia and T/Sgt.
George Rohbock from Utah were seasoned front-
line soldiers, in their 20's, who chose to
defend their country. I met these two men in
Sebring, Florida at different times. Their
story was so unique I decided to interview Roy
Gilbert.

This interview is June 23, 1992 in Sebring,
Florida and I'm talking to Roy Gilbert. We had
a mutual friend in Orem, Utah by the name of
George Rohbock. He and Roy were in German P.O.W.
Camps together during WWII.

George was on a mission for the L.D.S. Church
here in 1986 and '87 and by chance met Roy, who
owns Gilbert's Pharmacy, in Sebring.

One day George got up enough courage to go
in and inquire if this could be the same Roy
Gilbert.

They found that neither had discussed those
dark and cruel days they spent as Prisoners of
War and had placed it in the dark and forgotten
parts of their minds. They probably felt
failure as they both had been captured in battle
```

and experienced the humiliation of enemy treatment in miserable camps in Germany and Poland. Unknown to them at the time even a concentration camp where Jews were being exterminated.

Roy told of the unusual reunion with George after nearly fifty years. When they met he invited George into his office and told the store personnel not to disturb them for any reason.

They discussed the camps, the other prisoners, the trials they endured together such as the beatings, body lice and poor food which they had both tried to forget as if it never happened. Things they had not discussed since they were liberated at the end of the war.

It was a very emotional meeting as they found one would remember happenings that the other had dismissed from their minds and visa versa.

Roy had his Gideon Bible with some names he had written in it during the time they were prisoners of war. This helped George to remember names and events he had long since tried to forget.

Roy had a Masonic ring he wore during the war and to keep it from the Germans he pinned it to his closing under his arm. They were so lousy that no German guard would dare put their hand into a prisoner's armpit. This ring and the Gideon Bible were the only possessions that he retained through his P.O.W. ordeal.

He told about how cruel the Germans were to them. The food was terrible and they would threaten to execute them and stand them up before a firing squad, then pistol whip them into unconsciousness.

Roy told of a P.O.W. from Ohio that was with them whom he also met in Sebring. It seemed so unlikely that three P.O.W.'s, one from Georgia, one from Utah and one from Ohio could meet so many years later in Sebring, Florida.

The following is a tape recording by Roy:

This is June 23rd 1992 we are in Sebring, Florida. I lived in central Georgia and I left there for the Army February 1943.

After being processed in Atlanta, Georgia I was sent to Camp Walters, Texas which was an Infantry Replacement Training School (IRTS). It was to train replacement soldiers for both the Pacific and Europe.

While in Camp Walters I took my basic training which lasted 13 weeks. I remained there for an extra six weeks as a part of the Cadre to train more replacement soldiers.

I left Camp Walters in the latter part of the summer of 1943 for Ft. George G. Mead, Maryland and stayed there, on Cadre, still training for the invasion. I was there through the winter and in the spring I shipped out up to Massachusetts to Camp Miles Standish which was a kind of staging area. We were shipped out from there I believe in the latter part of May for Europe. We first went to Scotland and then down on to England.

By that time the invasion of the beaches were already on and by about the middle of June we went across the channel into the hedge rows and at that time was assigned to a different Army Group, I can't remember which group it was but it wasn't the Third Army because the Third Army had not been formed at that time.

While we were in the hedge row country on the edge of St. Lo, France, General George Patton came over and the 25th of July they formed what was to be known as the Third Army.

We moved out from the hedge rows which was mainly the rural area. We did hit some of the larger towns, Montargis, Oleans, LeMans and we wound up in Nancy, France.

In the interim while around Nancy I had been wounded twice, once on September 8th and again on November 29th, it was in the same forest is which we had been pushing forward to the Siegfried Line.

We had been at one time in the Siegfried but we pulled back and were hitting it again for the second time.

Now Gene asked me to tell about the capture.

It was on the morning of December 15th. I remember quite clearly, I was in the forward outpost checking on a machine gun placement in our lines. At this time a half track recon outfit pulled up and I asked the fellow, you all been to the top of the hill and they said yes. I said what's up there? He said ten thousand Germans. Well, you know we heard this kind of thing before.

What did us in, he said I'll tell you something else, "I just heard where they shot down Glenn Miller yesterday", this was on December 15, 1944 when Glenn Miller while crossing the channel was missing in action. We were more concerned in this than the fact that there were ten thousand Germans over the top of the hill.

Next morning we got up and were given orders to shove off. "K" Company ordered to be on the outer right and we would shove out and go into the woods and see what was in there.

Just before we shoved off, I looked up and there was an officer coming, a German SS officer, and he had two non-coms on either side and I said just look what we have here. He was just strolling across the top of this hill. There were no trees on this hill.

At this time the trees were on beyond where we were so I said to one of my key men, Rebel, who was also from Georgia, I said, "Rebel, we got to take that officer" so we shot the non-coms and the officer never moved. We ordered him to put his hands up above his head and to come in.

To make a long story short he was just carried away that we were there. He said, "I cannot believe this, you have by-passed my men. Did you not encounter my outfit?". I told him no way could we have by-passed his men. He said "Well I declare this is something else".

He spoke just as good of English as I did, probably better, so I said, what about this forest up ahead? He said nothing there, my men are back behind you all some way somehow.

I guess we did buy that tune so I said Ok boys and gave him to one of the men and said take him back.

We proceeded to cross this field, myself, Sgt Hendricks and Schwartz and Rebel were in the lead. Just before we got into the woods we heard cross fire and I looked back and saw most of my men were down in the field, whether they were shot or just took cover I will never know.

The four of us arrived into the wooded area into the forest. I looked to my right and I saw German soldiers in a trench and just as I raised my rifle Hendricks said "Gilbert, drop your gun". When he said this I dropped it with no hesitation. He said look to your left. I looked to my left and there was a German Sergeant and a machine gunner on the ground. The machine gunner was sited in on us.

I will always believe he was going to wait until I shot one of his men before he did anything in the world to us and I'm sure he would have cut us down. I looked back and I could see Hendricks and Schwartz but I couldn't see Rebel at that point. Hendricks and Schwartz had their hands up so we stood there and he kept hollering "surrender, surrender, surrender" and we said ya surrender.

We took another step and he came upon that gun and I thought, well he is going to kill us. I said we had surrendered so what's he talking about, we didn't have a dogs chance because the guy had already cocked the gun just waiting for us to shoot the first man. He was going to open up. Then I realized we had not knocked our helmets off so I said boys knock your helmets off. We knocked our helmets off and walked on in, and from there it was all down hill.

These fellows took us on in and there we were shaken down. Our gas masks, watches, and everything we had in our pockets such as cigarettes, candy bars, matches etc. were taken from us and there we were stripped down.

That night we were taken into a beautiful chateau where we were taken to the third floor. We stayed there for two days where we were fed and interrogated each night between 12 and 2 o'clock.

We were taken in one at a time and questioned and of course we gave our name, rank and serial number and this is all we were going to tell them. We told a couple of wild tales about how we crossed one of the rivers but whether they bought it or not we don't know.

We all stuck to our stories and it seems we all lived through that. Although we were threatened we were never beaten that night. Nobody was hurt there, they just threatened. Some German was playing an accordion or a concertina, I remember that quite well.

After two days there we moved on off. We were marched out and we tried once for an escape but this didn't pan out. They sent us back with two wounded soldiers. The three of us so far and we still had no account of where Rebel was.

One night later we were processed or taken into an abandoned factory of some kind and placed out in the center yard and the guards went off to the side and we tried to sleep.

Next morning we woke up and we saw this crippled German soldier along and he had an American soldier pushing a baby carriage. When we looked closer it was Rebel pushing the baby carriage with the radio in it. When he came in it put the four of us back together. We thought surly he had been shot but found he had not when we saw him coming in.

From there we wound up in a place I believe called Landau, I don't remember anything about Landau. From there we went on to Villingen which was about eighteen or twenty kilometers from Switzerland.

There we were placed into a barracks with a wood bunk thing without a mattress. I think this was about the third meeting I had with George

Rohbock. We had talked so much but I don't know if George was captured in the Bulge or like me just captured.

We figured that if we were to ever escape we had better do it there and there we made the one attempt to escape.

I have a report here that was written by John McGinnis who was in the crowd with us. I did not know John at this time.

I do remember we started an escape that was planned. I remember that night because I had a little duty there that I never could fulfill because it was all just jumbled all up as we didn't know our directions or anything else but we wanted to be out of that place. Anyway this attempted escape took place there and as McGinnis said the Germans caught us and they said that if anybody else tried to do it again they would kill Rohbock. Here they had picked him as a name to remember.

When there I met George and we became good friends right off the bat. He was the most unusual person, I don't know if the Germans liked him or respected him but they had strong feelings about him. They thought that he should have been fighting on the German side because his name was Rohbock. I don't think they ever got over that because it seemed they chose him to pick on.

Two more men tried an escape but they didn't shoot Rohbock, why I don't know. The Germans quickly chose George to pick on. They seemed to look at him as a traitor to their country or something. He told me later on that they took a dim view of him fighting with the Americans and thought he should be on the German side.

We remained there for a few days and left on a march. We found out later when they put us on a train we were in Heidelberg. On the march we only got a piece of black/brown bread once every twenty four hours to eat and no water unless you could find some snow or something else to chew on as there was not water or anything given to you at all.

I am sure that from Heidelberg we were on a train box car to the outskirts of Berlin, however we walked through Berlin. I don't remember how we got there but we wound up in Poland in a prison camp very near Stargard Staten. We stayed there a length of time however I can't remember dates so I don't know how long it was.

We left there because the Russians were coming in. I had seen them down below. The Germans got us out and lined us up. We decided, well we will kinda fall back and slack up if our allies were right down at the bottom of the mountain maybe they would overtake us.

We had two or three British boys with us that had been taken at Dunkirk and they said listen to us and stay with the SS. We said that under these conditions we were losing too many of our men but they said we would still be better off here than with those Russians. They said you will probably never see your country if you go with the Russians. Well I couldn't believe this at that time it seemed very strange to me but now I do believe it.

We were marched out of that camp and I don't even remember the name or number of it and we crossed the Oder River along with thousands and thousands of refugees.

After a while the SS had us in a different section marching us to Vandenberg which was about a nine day march. As I remember we left Stargard with about eleven hundred men and we wound up up with three or four hundred when we got to Vandenberg.

On this march I will go to my grave grateful to George Rohbock. My feet were bleeding the third or fourth day and I, like everyone else, was starving to death. We had that one little hunk of black bread each day. My feet were hurting me so bad and bleeding so bad that I just didn't see how I could go on so I told George that I was going to drop out now. He said oh no, you can't because you know that behind they have the killing squad back there. Anybody that is laying on the ground or sitting on the ground back there they are going to kill you. I said, well I just can't do it, y'all go on so I dropped down.

Jack Hargate told me recently that he and John had stopped and the guards nudged them on and told them to look forward straight ahead.

Jack said he heard a shot back there and was sure it was for me. Well it was back in the killing squad it wasn't where I was.

I was down on my knees when George Rohbock dropped down on his knees by me. I said George move on, move on with them as there is no way I'm going to make it. He said yes you are, you are going to make it. So he knelt there and he prayed and he said, Roy lets get up and I said I don't think so. In the interim of time one of the SS had come up on a bicycle or something back there. I told George he was on a bicycle and he said he was giving you the butt of his rifle on the back of your neck and head. I don't remember if he hit George or not but he mauled me pretty good several times in the back of my neck and then George just took my arm and pulled me up on my feet and I never went down again as I recall. So we just marched right on. Had George Rohbock not stopped and dropped down with me that day I wouldn't be here.

We arrived at the last prison camp that I was in which was named Sandbostel. Those were atrocious conditions. It was unbelievable what we saw and what we heard when we got there. Not only were there prisoners of war but there were what the Germans called the political prisoners, well they were the Jews.

When we first saw them they were in a loger between where we were staged and where we had to go for that rotten soup every day at noon. We had to go by there loger and we just kept looking at these people in these striped suits and we just didn't know who they were.

We questioned the regular guards because you couldn't question the SS about anything. We asked them who these people were and they said they were criminals and they were murders and they were rapists and everything bad you could think of.

Then we noticed the star of David. And of course this was part of the final solution. Each day as we went for our soup we would look across at these people. I don't think there was one there that weighed 75 or 80 pounds. They were fed in a trough about like we feed hogs in Georgia.

I don't know what they were given but even if they were given the rotten soup we were given they couldn't have weighed very much as all of us were down then unbelievably down.

Each day as we went by we would watch these people and look at them. I don't believe that many of them had much sense, I think at that time they just did not know what was going on at all. Then one day we saw a column of them coming across this field. Well it was just another group from some concentration camp somewhere that had been almost overrun and they pulled them out and were bringing them over to Sandbostal.

So they jammed all these people in there and I thought it was a total of twenty two thousand of these political prisoners in this one compound. It was an enormous number of people in there and there were some young people among them and some small children. We just couldn't understand but anyway before long they put to killing these people. They killed a great number of them with guns and guns and guns.

One day when George was here we were talking about this thing he asked if I remembered the charcoal pit down by the kitchen where he went for the soup. I said, George I do but I hadn't thought about it since then. There was an enormous pit filled with, what looked to us like, charcoal and they had thrown a number of these Jews into this pit and they had others laying around the edge who were dead or dying and we still could not put it together as to just what these people were doing.

There was no place in the world worse than Sandbostal, the soup was getting thinner and most of the time it had maggots in it but we ate it on and on.

Finally we got a Red Cross parcel we had been promised Red Cross parcels all along and we finally got one. I remember getting two of them while at Sandbostal. A parcel was shared by two prisoners so George and I shared one and Jack and John shared one. John writes how George made a cake out of some of the things in the parcel and I do remember that.

There isn't too much more I remember about Sandbostel as by that time I was real bad. We all had dysentery terribly and mine was getting worse and there was nothing we could do for it. I finally got to where I could not get up and walk. In the interim, I learned recently from Jack and George that those who could get up and walk had been taken away to another camp from where we were.

The town was called Westertimke. George had recognized the name from a write-up I have in a Belgian paper here. He told me this is where we were liberated and I said no we were liberated in Sandbostel. For some reason I had forgotten that George, Jack and John had been moved out and I stayed there and I was left with the dead and probably the dying and maybe I just didn't realize it at that time.

But I didn't die, apparently I got a little bit stronger because about the 29th of April, and these boys had been gone about two weeks because they were liberated earlier than we were at Sandbostel. They too were liberated by the British and I believe the name of that outfit was...but anyway one of the British guys there in the camp came to me and said do you feel strong enough to come out here with me? I said oh yeah and I said where are the loger guards, the guards inside? And he said man, they are gone. And I said what's coming off then, what do you think?

I had heard heavy gun fire before that and he said come here I want to show you something. He had me get up on a box or something and he said look over on that hillside and what do you see Gilbert? I said my God we're going to be liberated. Those are American tanks. He said what's those red things on them? I said they are orange panels, they mark the lines on the back of all our tanks. However they weren't American tanks, they were British tanks and I didn't know what it was on a British tank.

That was on the 29th and like I said the guns had been firing and in the interim what the Germans had done was turned these Jews out into the main Stieloger road and were firing their guns on them. They would kill them until their guns got hot and they would stop for them to cool off and they would fire again to kill more. As I remember I was told before I left there they had killed about eleven thousand of these people and they had them all piled up in the middle of the road when I left the place.

Before this, this was on the 29th that the guns started firing, and it was about 2:00 o'clock in the afternoon on the 30th of April that the guard's armored division pulled on into camp and took the surrender. All that was left was a few of the staff officers out front and they took surrender of the camp.

I was there about two days more trying to do, with what strength I had, trying to sort out the boys who were dead and get their dog tags and those things.

Then I noticed in the main loger road these piles and piles of bodies. Well the British had gone into this town down below and I can't remember the name of that town and had brought a bunch of civilians, said they were nurses and doctors and all, to pile these dead bodies up.

That is the last thing I remember when I went out the gate to get in a truck to leave that place. The last thing was looking back and seeing these tremendous piles of dead bodies.

I remember George saying to me sometime before the surrender or the end of this whole ordeal, we were so down and out, starving and discouraged, George looked and me and he said: "Here, we can no longer kill these people, the only way we can beat them is to live."

(Transcribed by Gene V. Sorensen from a taped interview with some additions from personal conversations with Roy Gilbert)

OUR GIFT

My Afterthoughts - We have all heard the term "sly like a fox." Well, that German SS officer may not have been sly like a fox getting caught out like that, but psychologically, he was *very* sly. Wow! Dad said that he was as cool as he could be and didn't flinch when the shots rang out, and the guys on each side of him dropped. When ordered to come forward, he did so with no resistance. I think this guy had been around the block quite a few times, seasoned as they say, and *really* battle-hardened not to flinch.

He seemed to be just numb to it all and started right out chatting away with Dad and the guys like nothing had just happened. This not only shows his coolness, but I think it was part of his plan as he needed to try to establish trust. Well, this he did. Dad said, "he spoke just as good English as I did, probably better."

I got a feeling this SS officer was highly educated and a bit older than Dad and his guys. I would guess he had studied American culture. I believe he knew the different accents of Americans and the terminology they commonly use. Why? Because of *one* phrase in a sentence from the SS officer. "Well, I declare, this is something else." *Well, I declare?* What are the odds of him using that phrase in his everyday vocabulary? I can guarantee you that was the first time that line ever came out of any SS officer's mouth. He knew Dad was from the South and possibly even Georgia.

Dad had the "classically distinct" Georgia accent, and this officer sure picked up on using it to his advantage. This SS officer could have won an Oscar award because Dad said, "I guess we bought that tune." He knew what awaited them in that forest the whole time. I know that in my early 20s, as Dad was then, I was a lot more "trusting" of people than I am now. Don't get me wrong, I've got many people I can trust, but by your 60s, you learn to read people better and you are more aware of those you can't. Until I found this interview, I had never known about the "I declare" line. If I had known about it before Dad passed away, I would have asked, "Didn't it sound funny with a German accent?" I don't think I've ever heard it without a slow, Southern drawl.

LIBERATION
Dad's Original Writing Transcribed

We were liberated from Sandbostel on April 29, 1945, by a unit of British guards around Dresden. Two or three days later, after being deloused and given new clothing, we were flown from an airfield nearby to Brussels, Belgium by British pilots and C-47 planes. In Brussels, we were checked over to some extent by American doctors. I remember some controversy concerning my status as a POW. I was never issued by the Germans a loger number or "dog tag". This "dog tag" was a piece of lead with a number on it. Why I did not have the loger number is another story. I won't go into this at this time. I had my dog tag. What's the big deal? I went over to Americans to explain why. After a time, someone came to me and said, "You are indeed an American soldier." I can't remember what they had done to confirm this. Maybe I never did know. I wasn't too worried. I was out of the hands of the SS and back with my people from Brussels. We went to a "tent city" on the coast of France. Whether we went by train or truck I can't remember. The name of the "tent city" was Camp Lucky Strike. Nearby were Camp Cornell and Camp Chesterfield. At Camp Lucky Strike and while in Brussels we were fed about 6 small meals a day, drip coffee and cake. We all had been POW's. While we were here Germany signed surrender papers.

18

THE LIBERTY SHIP HOMECOMING

The following story was handwritten in pencil by Dad a long time ago; although it has faded over the years, we could make out most of it. In Dad's own words, this story describes his time on the Liberty Ship coming home and his transfer to Camp Kilman, NJ.

Writing Transcribed:

We set sail on a Liberty ship from somewhere in France. Soon, there were 15 or 20 Liberty ships in our convoy. I put in for the disc jockey and got the job. I didn't know exactly where my "studio" would be, but it turned out to be high above the deck. I played Glenn Miller, Tommy Dorsey, Jimmy Dorsey, Les Brown, and all of the Doris Day records that I could find. My selection seemed to have satisfied the guys. If it hadn't, I would have heard from them. Lifeboat drills came off 2-3 times a day.

I suppose there was some doubt that the U-boats knew the war was over or not. We POWs were the color of lemons. Jaundiced to the hilt. I could sit up there and work my turntable and still be in the sun. Therefore, I almost stayed naked all of the time, trying to change from yellow to tan. One day, the Captain or Commander or whatever shouted, "Lifeboats!" This meant getting your life jacket and lining up on deck. On this day, I decided to stay put. I had had enough drills, and besides, he couldn't see me. He kept shouting, "That means everyone!" I thought...sure it does... Then I heard, "You up there in the studio, get down here *now*!!" Boy! I hit that deck in 2 seconds, all in my under shorts and life jacket. How he saw me, I don't know. I remember a PX, but there was no food, candy, or anything to eat. We still had those 6 little meals a day. The big thing was we were told that we would get steak and ice cream when we got to the States.

23 days after sailing from France, we arrived in New York Harbor. The decks were always slippery with throw-up. Someone shouted, "There she is!" referring to the Statue of Liberty, and we all filed out on deck. There was a poor soldier near me who slipped on the slippery deck and fell, apparently breaking his legs. He just lay there crying, thinking I am sure if you live through all that he had in Europe, to come home and do this. Counting the 2 days that we stayed in the POW camp, the time in Brussels, and the 23 days on the Atlantic, it must have been the very last of May when we got to NY.

From NY, we were transported to Camp Kilman, NJ. Ice cream and steak we did get. After this, we got the 3 meals a day, along with whatever we wanted from PX. I remember 2 things that happened while at Kilman. One, when I was in the PX, a female employee called over to me. Seeing my 35th Division emblem, she asked what regiment and then what Battalion. I told her this.

Then she said, "My husband was in that outfit, but he is not coming back." No fault of hers, but these were cutting words for me. I don't remember how I handled this. The other incident happened when I was walking down the street, and a soldier on the second-story little porch yelled, "Hey, Sergeant, hold up!" He came down and asked if I recognized him. I told him that I did not. Then he said that he had been in my platoon and that I had sent him on patrol, but he never came back to us. After some talking and thinking, I did indeed remember the time and place. I remember not the soldier. Our objective at that time was Mortain. A battalion of the 30th Infantry was surrounded at Mortain, and we were on our way to get to them. The time was August of '44. Fighting had been hard, and our strength was short. On that particular night, I had picked 3 new replacements to slip out on a listening patrol. I usually didn't do this, but our other soldiers were worn out. I explained to them how they were to crawl to the first hedgerow in front of us to listen and if it seemed clear of Krauts to crawl to one more....one...no more. Away they went.

After too much time had passed, I realized that something had happened. I had Rebel to sit on the hedgerow that we were in and watch me as I went out to see about the Patrol. I went to the first row and heard nothing. I went to the second row, and as I got there, the Germans put on what we called a "screaming counterattack." This wasn't an attack at all. What they would do would be to gap up one row from where they were and run and scream back up to their original position. We had learned this trick, so this was no big deal. However, this did put me in a very awkward situation. Nothing but an 8-to-10-foot hedgerow between me and the enemy.

Now, I knew that there was a railroad running near both hedgerows. I had seen it before dark. I made my way to this railroad. Crossed it and got on a path that paralleled it. It was not a dark night. I knew that I was not far from our line, and although I couldn't see him, I knew that Rebel was still in position on the hedgerow. I would have to cross that railroad to get back to the platoon. Before I crossed, I saw a hog pen and what looked like a mound of dirt. All of this was to my left as I proceeded toward our line.

Just before I started to cross the tracks, Rebel shouted to me, "Gilbert, look behind you!" I was lying flat on my stomach. I rolled over and held my rifle on this soldier. Enough to see that he was in GI uniform, but his rifle was strung in a strange manner. Strap on one shoulder with strap crossing the chest and butt of the rifle on the other side of the body. I said, "What outfit are you from?"

He replied, "Hello," and just stood there. I was not prepared for something like this. This man was in the same uniform as I was.

I remember shouting, "Boy, you had better speak up!" At that time, he turned to run, and I saw his Kraut mess kit on the back of his belt. Rebel and I shot about the same time. I relayed this story to the soldier. He said that he knew most of what happened on this day. The Patrol had been captured. I don't remember the details of their capture. I do remember that he said that they had seen me. They had been stripped of uniform, and they were in those mounds of dirt that I had seen. I believe they were potato hills. Anyway, the German who had confronted me was wearing one of their uniforms. This is about all that I remember about Camp Kilman except for my call home. I had gotten some letters from Mama in the summer of '44. Now, this was about 10 months later. I was just afraid that something may have happened during this time. I learned later that all they knew was the telegram they received from the War Department which stated: *Wounded in Action*

1. Returned in Action
2. Wounded in Action
3. Returned to Action
4. Missing in Action

OUR GIFT

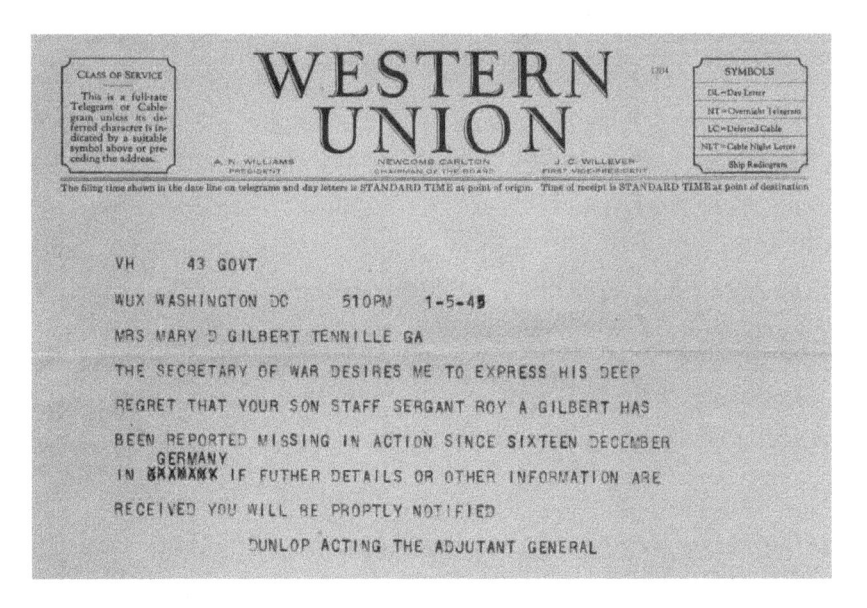

```
VH      43 GOVT
WUX WASHINGTON DC      510PM   1-5-45
MRS MARY D GILBERT TENNILLE GA
THE SECRETARY OF WAR DESIRES ME TO EXPRESS HIS DEEP
REGRET THAT YOUR SON STAFF SERGANT ROY A GILBERT HAS
BEEN REPORTED MISSING IN ACTION SINCE SIXTEEN DECEMBER
   GERMANY
IN BXXMXKX IF FUTHER DETAILS OR OTHER INFORMATION ARE
RECEIVED YOU WILL BE PROPTLY NOTIFIED
       DUNLOP ACTING THE ADJUTANT GENERAL
```

My Afterthoughts: The one thing that was hard to figure out was the name our guys gave for the tactic the Germans used while fighting in the hedgerows with us. Dad and the guys had gotten used to this tactic and realized it was just a trick. It was a cat-and-mouse game where the Germans would try to lure our guys out or at least give up their position by returning fire to a spot the Germans had evacuated by running back to their original position instead of a forward-charging attack. This was my best guess, "a screaming counterattack?" Sounds kind of strange.

I wish I could ask Dad. When I read the part of the story where the German dressed in our uniform was confronted by Dad, he just said, "Hello."

I just said, "Wow!" That sure triggered a memory. I had forgotten about that. I now remembered Dad imitating the German's voice saying that. I must have been quite young when I heard that for the first time because of the low tone and accent Dad used. It kind of creeped me out. Dad did a great imitation. Thank God Rebel was there to give Dad a heads-up! That's one example of Rebel being at the right place at the right time.

19

FROM HELL TO HEAVEN

Just think of the contrast from experiencing one of the worst "death camps" over there to find yourself on the upper deck of one of our Liberty ships being disc jockey.

Remember the descriptions Dad gave of the sights, sounds, and smells of that last hell camp he was in? That last camp was as close to hell as it gets for a person on our planet at that point in time in history. Now, just think of sitting on the upper deck of that ship in the sunshine, playing your favorite music. Think of those sights, sounds, and smells!

Think of the site of 15 to 20 other Liberty ships around you cutting through the waves of the Atlantic Ocean, all heading HOME to New York. The wind in your face and the fresh smell of salt air. I guess Dad's favorite song was Midnight Serenade by Glen Miller. I heard it a thousand times at home on our stereo as a kid, usually when Dad was mopping our terrazzo floors. I can see Dad playing that song on the ship, gazing across that ocean and thinking, I'm alive, thank God, I'm alive! They all were just now realizing that they had accomplished what, at times, must have seemed impossible and that they had defeated the evilest force on the planet. From the four months in prison camps, Dad had been starved down from 190 lbs. to maybe 130 lbs. I'm sure from the small meals they were getting on the ship, he could feel his body coming back to life, probably like being reborn. Just think how he felt after dodging death as many times as he did that now he had a very real second chance at life. I'm sure that on that 23-day trip across the Atlantic, the sunrise, sunset, moon, and stars never looked as beautiful.

20

PHONE CALL THAT ANSWERED MANY PRAYERS

Dad's handwritten document transcribed of his first phone call home after his release in Late May or early June 1945

Miss Bessie knew the happenings in Tennille like the back of her hand. She knew who was out of town and most likely when they had gone. How did she have all of the up-to-date information? She listened in on most all telephone conversations, and it was not at all unusual for her to enter the conversations.

Miss Bessie Hartley was the daytime telephone operator in Tennille.

The Liberty Ship, which was filled with Ex POWs, arrived in New York harbor, and we were transported by train to Camp Kilman in New Jersey. I had been at Kilman for 2 or 3 days before making the call to Tennille. Not knowing just what Mama and Mimi, (my grandmother), knew about my situation. I had to be cautious. I was never a registered prisoner of war. I had no longer number, therefore, I was never registered as a POW with the International Red Cross in Geneva. I had to make the call, and I had all the confidence that Miss Bessie could help me do that. I asked the NJ operator to get me Tennille, and as I had hoped, Miss Bessie answered:

"Miss Bessie? This is Roy Jr."

"Roy Jr? We thought you had been killed."

"No, Miss Bessie, I have been a POW."

"Roy Jr, William (Who is my brother and had also been listed as Missing in Action) is at home now, and he has been a POW."

"Miss Bessie, I want to talk to Mama, not Mimi."

You see, not knowing what they knew, the excitement of Mimi hearing my voice may be too much. Miss Bessie was true to form. She said that William was buying Mama a new dress and that she was at the Happ & Parris Department store in Sandersville at this time. So, it was in the dress department of Happ & Parris's Department store that Mama learned that I was alive and well.

OUR GIFT

21

WHAT REALLY HAPPENED TO REBEL

I've often wondered what REALLY happened to Rebel. Dad's story concerning Rebel when they were captured was, "As he entered the woods, he could not see the three of us. He was probably not in the woods when the firing in the field occurred." Obviously, Dad and his men were not fired upon. Rebel most likely heard them being captured, even if he couldn't see them, and decided to hang back. I think after Rebel had the encounter with the German soldier, then played 'Houdini' disappearing into that hole, while hiding out from the Germans, gave him a little time to think. I believe that Rebel was captured a short time after Dad and his men ONLY because he wanted to be. Why do I think this? I heard several times over the years Dad say, "Rebel always said he would never be taken alive." Rebel and my Dad had such a strong bond and I don't think he could stand being alone and not knowing what was going to happen to them. He could have just stayed hidden but the love and loyalty he had for my Dad was greater than even the concern for his own life. I remember Dad telling me something about Rebel when they were marched to Stalag VB at Villingen and separated. I guess they learned to read each other pretty well. Dad said, "As they separated us and were shoving us off, we looked at each other for the last time and I just had a bad feeling. We didn't get very far down the road and I heard the shot."

Dad never talked much about that. I am just assuming that the look on Rebel's face and his telling Dad several times, "They'll never take me alive," gave Dad no doubt that the shot was for Rebel. As Dad said in one of the writings, they left him for dead.

When I started writing this book I wondered about Rebel. What really happened to him? I knew Rebel's real name was Delmar Stafford and I often wondered if Rebel may still be alive. Shelley started researching military records and found both my Dad's and Delmar Stafford's (Rebel) military records online from the WWII data file. Although my Dad and Delmar Stafford had similar military entry records, ie; Branch, Report dates, Unit numbers, Area, Organization, etc., no POW camp was listed for Delmar Stafford leading us to believe he was never taken Prisoner of War. I'm thinking, could this have been Rebel and he didn't get killed in action after all?

Shelley found an obituary of Delmar Stafford who passed away in 2011 and the memorial service took place at a funeral home in Alpena, Michigan. The obituary also stated he was born in Michigan in 1925, however, Dad always said that Rebel was from Georgia. We contacted the funeral home and were connected to several family members to try and determine if this Delmar Stafford ever lived in Georgia. The few family members we spoke to were very nice and were more than willing to help but unfortunately, we couldn't determine if this was the same "Rebel", nor could they. Nothing seemed to add up.

Upon further research, we found another Delmar Stafford who was born in Georgia in 1920. We contacted a local historian who connected us to Delmar Stafford's cousin who still resides in Georgia. He was extremely pleasant; however, he doesn't remember much about Delmar other than him being in WWII, as he was only 6 years old when Delmar died. He told us Delmar passed away in 1957 in a car accident and had no other living relatives. That would make him only 37 years old when he passed away.

We feel mixed emotions from the bits of information we have gathered, however, his profile lines up with his character. In a perfect scenario, I would have loved to have talked to a relative or friend young enough that Delmar would have discussed his military experience with. All I would have had to have heard was Dad's name mentioned or Delmar's nickname, Rebel.

With all this aside, we concluded that we had found our true "Rebel" from Georgia. Although his life was cut short, the memories Dad shared with us of "Rebel was the best soldier I ever fought alongside", will never be forgotten. In our eyes, Rebel is a legend and will live on forever.

22

POST-WAR

I've often thought about the hardships Dad went through, from the time he was born until after the war, and then what a great life he has had since.

After the war, Dad attended college at the University of Georgia College of Pharmacy where he met my Mom, Ann Burkett. They got married and later moved to Sebring in 1953, built a beautiful home on Lake Jackson, and had four children, Dianne, Larry, Terri, and myself.

OUR GIFT

In 1959 he opened up Gilbert Drugs, in Sebring, Florida, where he was the only pharmacist that offered delivery of medications any time of day or night. As I stated in a previous chapter, I accompanied him on many of those night deliveries. Gilbert Drugs was originally located on Ridgewood Drive and the local teenagers would hang out there after school in the soda fountain area.

ROBERT GILBERT

I still have great memories of that drugstore. My best memories were cherry cokes, thick milkshakes, and the tuna and egg salad sandwiches Bea and Hazel made at the counter. They were so thick you could hardly get your mouth around them.

"GILBERT DRUGS WOODEN NICKELS" were given out as tokens for free coffee or coke. You can speak to any local, longtime resident of Sebring and they are sure to remember Gilbert Drugs and my Dad. Browse through the Facebook posts on Home Sweet Sebring and you will still find many endearing memories and posts about my father.

On top of operating Gilbert Drugs, my Dad was very involved in the community. He was a City Councilman from 1962 until 1967, director of the Chamber of Commerce, and named chairman during his last year. From there he took up duties with the Utilities Commission passing through the proper offices of commissioner, assistant secretary, secretary vice chairman, and chairman. Upon his retirement, he was presented with a plaque, along with some kind and appreciative words for his many services to the city of Sebring.

Dad passed away in 2006 from complications following a kidney stone operation. He had a rock garden of them through the years after the war. The operation itself went fine as the doctor removed it by the cystoscope method. This was the largest one Dad ever had; passing it naturally wasn't possible. Dad put this operation off for two to three weeks with intentions of trying to make it through the Christmas holidays and not disrupt this time of year for everyone though we all didn't care. This was just Dad's way, always thinking of others first. The stress on Dad during this time was the straw that broke the camel's back. His body had already been weakened through the years from a disease called spinocerebellar ataxia, the dying of the spinal cord brought on by severe trauma. It was the beating he took on that march to Sandbostel you read about and Dad never took a dime from the government. The beating damaged the vertebrae in the cervical area. As the fractured vertebrae healed, they grew spurs that put pressure on and slowly sawed into the spinal cord. That explains the headaches he would get from time to time over the years. In 1988, Shands Hospital in Gainesville, Florida, performed an operation in which they removed the damaged vertebrae replacing them with cadaver bone. The good part was the headaches were gone but the damage was already done to the spinal cord itself long ago and the disease continues to progress. This disease causes a person to eventually lose all voluntary muscle control. He went from a cane to a walker and eventually a wheelchair. I remember when he was first diagnosed with this, I overheard him in another room talking to Mom and he said, "Well, Ann, they got me!" The emotion I heard in his voice with the next line punched me in the gut. "Those bastards finally got me!" I thought about all the good he had done for everyone all of his life and how physically active he has always been and now, THIS! Really? I just looked at Dad and said "You know, it just doesn't seem fair…" That's all I got out when Dad looked me straight in the eyes and said TWO WORDS, "Never question." With the tone he used, I never did. I ended up helping take care of him for years after that until his passing.

ROBERT GILBERT

Roy Gilbert

1922-2006

OUR GIFT

23

HITTING THE DECK - SIX FLAGS

I remember it was around 1965 or 1966. Our family went on a vacation that summer to the Smoky Mountains. We decided to go to Six Flags Over Georgia one day, and as we entered the park, we were walking on a wooden deck in front of the country stores on each side of the street, simulating an old Western town. We were in single file due to the amount of people on the boardwalk.

My Dad was about twenty feet in front of my brother and me, along with my mom and two sisters who were in between us. Suddenly, my heart jumped out of my chest, and I'm sure a lot of others did too, as there was no warning as to what was happening. The Cowboys began a "mock" shootout in the street. The gunshots were loud due to the amplifying effects of the buildings and the canopy overhead. One cowboy was right in front of us, firing away. I noticed the commotion ahead. I was only six or seven years old, so though it was hard to see, I noticed the crowd up ahead on the boardwalk parting to the sides, and people were looking down. Dad just suddenly appeared in the middle of them. I remember him half laughing and saying something to the on-lookers. When I caught up to them, I asked Dad what happened. As we started walking back right away, he just kind of chuckled, shaking his head, and said, "Boy, I hit the deck!"

Mom was trying to make light of the situation where Dad got a little embarrassed, I think. She said to us, "he thought he was back in the war being shot at."

She made some comment about how he just disappeared by going down and flattening out so fast. Though Mom was smiling and kind of laughing, I could tell by the tone of her voice she was getting a little emotional. It's amazing how the brain works. How many times do you figure Dad dropped down and saved his life by "hitting the deck" in combat? Though totally subconscious, it is a survival reflex that never turned off, still on alert twenty years later.

OUR GIFT

24

GENERAL PATTON
A LEGACY OF LEADERSHIP

Patton, Flying West, Hopes to Fight in Pacific

(Pictures on Page 17)

BOSTON, June 8.—(P)—General George S. Patton Jr., hoping he is on his way to "fight the Japanese," left the Bedford Airport for Los Angeles Friday, taking off before most of the million people who gave him a hero's welcome Thursday had gone to work.

The dynamic, gun-toting chief of the invincible Third Army—stirred by the welcome of his adopted state upon his first return to the United States from the war in Europe, told newsmen, "I sincerely hope I fight the Japanese."

The general was accompanied by Mrs. Patton. They will stop at Denver, Col., where they will be accorded a reception.

"My ambition," he said in an interview, "is to get to the Pacific, but it may not be fulfilled."

"Can't Be Quoted"

He declined to amplify his remark but said "a general officer can not be quoted as to the possibilities of his assignments."

The 59-year-old four-star general talked briefly with newsmen after one of the most tumultuous receptions in the city's history.

Patton said he hoped to get a week or ten-day leave, which he would like to spend with his sister in Los Angeles.

"There is a little church out there where I was baptized and confirmed," he said. "God has been very good to me and I'd like to go there to give thanks to Him."

The church is St. Gabriel's Episcopal Church.

Patton said it was hard for him to talk about the Third Army "because when I start out on the Third Army I get incoherent."

Patton also praised the "magnificent reception" given him by the people of Massachusetts.

The brilliant Third Army general was welcomed by shouting throngs estimated at more than a million people, after a transatlantic flight from Paris via Newfoundland.

Crowds lined the parade route from Bedford Airport to Boston and a vast multitude heard him speak briefly from the hatch shell on the Charles River esplanade before he attended a state dinner.

Some 400 wounded veterans of the Third Army sat in a reserved section in front of the shell and all during his speech the general looked directly at the men who had fought with him in North Africa and Europe.

"With your blood and bonds we crushed the Germans before they got here," he said.

"This ovation is not for me, George S. Patton. George S. Patton is simply a hook on which to hang the Third Army."

He said it was a popular idea that a man was a hero when he was killed, but Patton said, "a man is frequently a fool when he gets killed."

"These men are the heroes," he added, looking at his Third Army wounded. Then he saluted the veterans and walked from the platform.

At the state dinner the general praised his generals and the enlisted men who served under him.

"I speak of the men who, regardless of mud, regardless of ice, regardless of snow, went on and on," he said.

"These men were heroic Americans—and they are heroic.

"We should thank God such men were born.

"I can't say any more," he added, wiping tears from his eyes.

101

PATTON NEWSPAPER ARTICLE TRANSCRIBED

PATTON, FLYING WEST, HOPES TO FIGHT IN PACIFIC

BOSTON, June 8, 1945 (AP) – General George S. Patton Jr., hoping he is on his way to "fight the Japanese," left the Bedford Airport for Los Angeles Friday – taking off before most of the million people who gave him a heroes welcome Thursday had gone to work. The dynamic, gun-toting chief of the invincible Third Army-stirred by the welcome of his adopted state upon his first return to the United States from the war in Europe, told newsmen, "I sincerely hope I fight the Japanese".

The general was accompanied by Mrs. Patton. They will stop at Denver, Col., where they will be accorded a reception.

My ambition, "he said in an interview, "is to get to the Pacific, but it may not be fulfilled."

"Can't Be Quoted"

He declined to amplify his remark but said "a general officer cannot be quoted as to the possibilities of his assignments".

The 59-year-old four-star general talked briefly with newsmen after one of the most tumultuous receptions in the city's history.

Patton said he hoped to get a week or ten-day leave, which he would like to spend with his sister in Los Angeles.

"There is a little church out there where I was baptized and confirmed," he said. "God has been very good to me and I'd like to go there to give thanks to Him."

The church is St. Gabriel's Episcopal Church.

Patton said it was hard for him to talk about the Third Army "because when I start out on the Third Army I get incoherent."

Patton also praised the "magnificent reception" given him by the people of Massachusetts.

The brilliant Third Army general was welcomed by shouting throngs estimated at more than a million people, after a transatlantic flight from Paris via Newfoundland.

Crowds lined the parade route from Bedford Airport to Boston and a vast multitude heard him speak briefly from the hatch shell on the Charles River esplanade before he attended a state dinner.

Some 400 wounded veterans of the Third Army sat in a reserved section in front of the shell and all during his speech the general looked directly at the men who had fought with them in North Africa and Europe.

"With your blood and bonds we crushed the Germans before they got here," he said.

"This ovation is not for me, George S. Patton. George S. Patton is simply a hook on which to hang the Third Army."

He said it was a popular idea that a man was a hero when he was killed, but Patton said, "a man is frequently a fool when he gets killed."

"These men are the heroes," he added, looking at his Third Army wounded. Then he saluted the veterans and walked from the platform.

At the state dinner the general praised his generals and the enlisted men who served under him.

"I speak of the men who, regardless of mud, regardless of ice, regardless snow, went on and on," he said.

"These men were heroic Americans-and they are heroic.

"We should thank God such men were born".

"I can't say any more," he added, wiping tears from his eyes.

General George S. Patton

George Smith Patton Jr. was a general in the United States Army who commanded the Seventh Army in the Mediterranean Theater of World War II, and the Third Army in France and Germany after the Allied invasion of Normandy in June 1944.

This book would not be complete without mentioning General George S. Patton. General Patton was a brilliant but hot-tempered U.S. Army general who was arguably the Allies' most gifted tank commander.

OUR GIFT

There was NO general that my father would have wanted more to have called the shots and led them into battle other than THIS man. He had their TRUST and their RESPECT.

I found this newspaper article in my dad's archives, which was printed in 1945 on General George Patton and although I am no expert on the general's life, this article tells us a lot, as short as it is. He was religious, loved his men, and cursed like a sailor. Sources such as the movie Patton with George C. Scott enlightened us to how much of a historian he was. He seemed to know every detail of every battle ever fought in this world which made him a GREAT tactician. Remember the line in Patton where he was watching Rommel and his battalion coming across the desert, Patton and his battalion were ready and waiting. As the tank battle took place Patton was getting the upper hand and as he was watching through binoculars said, "Rommel, you magnificent bastard, I read your book!" He loved the challenge of war and I feel that he was born for this purpose. Patton believed in signs, such as a time a bomb went off close to where he was standing spraying shrapnel everywhere, and he didn't get a scratch. He saw this as a sign that he was to go on to bigger and better things. He also believed in reincarnation and that he had fought in major battles that took place thousands of years ago. I'm sure General Patton was chomping at the bit to go on to Japan. What I find intriguing about this article is the last to read it were totally unaware of what was coming. When we dropped the atomic bombs on Hiroshima and Nagasaki, the war was over and the world changed forever. I wonder what General Patton thought about that. Would he have felt obsolete? He also did not trust and hated Russia. He wanted to take captured German soldiers, go in, and take the country. That made the politician's heads explode. General Patton was as far from politically correct as you can get as he seemed to have no filter. He stuck his foot in his mouth quite often like towards the end of this article. When he was speaking from the Shel in Boston, and said, "It was a popular idea that a man was a hero when he was killed but a man is frequently a fool when he gets killed." Oh boy, I bet that line raised some eyebrows. Those 400 wounded men sitting before him knew exactly what he meant, as well as any veteran who has experienced combat since then. The public, however, does not. At times, during the heat of battle with hell raining down, human beings, out of panic can do illogical or what some would be considered stupid things. Patton probably witnessed men in battle running from what was considered a safe spot, like a foxhole, trying to find a safer spot and get killed. No soldier is immune from this, by the way. General Patton probably witnessed this so many times, his grief turned to anger and that is most likely why he used the word "fool." Love him, hate him, or a little of both, ALL respected him, especially the enemy. Unless General Patton was ready and waiting for the enemy to come to him and surprise them, once he took the offensive and started his move, HANG ON! His main tactic seemed to be to move out and keep moving as fast as possible. Do not stop and plow over anything that gets in your way. Once the enemy is engaged, hit them hard and when possible, keep pushing in. Always take the offensive and never dig in. The idea is to not give them a chance to think, set up, regroup, or breathe. It's like two prize fighters going at it with no bell. Overwhelming the enemy was the goal. Wow! That tires me out just thinking about it. Somehow, no matter how tired, how hungry, or how hot or cold these guys were, they had that extra gear. They were INCREDIBLY tough. Modern-day language could respectfully refer to them as "true badasses". True heroes and true Americans they were. It is easy to see how Patton loved them. At the end of General Patton's

speech, at the state dinner, he said of the men enlisted under him, "We should thank God such men were born. I can't say anymore," he added, wiping tears from his eyes. We as Americans thank God General Patton was born and pray for more like him to emerge.

25

LAST CHAPTER

Well, now that the book is done, I asked myself the question, "How do I feel about it?" It's a very strange mix of emotions. I am, of course, very happy and relieved at the same time that it is *documented*. Remember how I said if something happened to me, these stories would die with me. I was absolutely thrilled to have found the tape and the other papers Dad had written. What an irreplaceable bonus. The ones mom wrote while Dad told of the encounters were easy to read because she had beautiful handwriting. On the other hand, while some of Dad's writings were readable, trying to decipher and figure out some of it could put you in the "loony bin".

I said I had mixed emotions about the book, and one is regret. At first, I regretted that I didn't ask Dad if he could remember the location of where each one of these stories took place. Mapping his path would have been awesome, and all of those years I took care of him, you would have thought I would have, in fact, thought to ask him just that. That is just the way life goes. *However*, finding "The Interview" was a *huge bonus* that more than makes up for that. I remember a comment Dad made quite often through the years concerning a particular canon the Germans would use against us. He would say, "Boy, those 88's were hell!"

I never really thought much of it until after he passed away, and I found out what they were capable of and their incredibly destructive power. Wow! I guess they were hell! Now, I wish I had asked him how close he was to the detonations. One regret for sure would be that

OUR GIFT

I didn't get to read these papers Dad wrote before he passed away. That way he could have told us what some of the words were that drove us nuts trying to figure out. My other regret that will be with me for life is not being able to talk to a member of Rebel's family about what an important asset he was to Dad during that war. "His number one Scout."

Another emotion I felt was sadness about what had happened to our country. Writing this book caused me to flashback to a time when life just seemed more innocent, simple, and pure. If the little town of Sebring was a microcosm of the way the majority of the people treated each other in this country, we were in a good place. I was born in 1959, and as I grew up, I couldn't help but notice how my dad's generation treated each other. Even those who were too young or old to go to war knew they were truly blessed to have been on the right side of history and could live normal, free lives. For most people of that generation, their word was everything. Deals were made with a handshake. They were proud to be American and loved their country. I think it's human nature to love and appreciate something that matters even more when you know it could have been lost forever.

Most of this generation went to church or at least tried to follow the Ten Commandments. They just wanted to live decent lives in peace with fellow Americans and take care of their families. As I have said, Dad died in 2006, and many times, I have thought, if Dad were to pop back in front of me right now, *how* would I explain to him what's going on in our country in 2023? WHERE would I even begin? I have a vision of how he might respond. He would stare at me with the "deer in the headlights look" for sure, and with some of the things I would tell him, he would probably wonder if I had lost my mind.

Seriously, it would break his heart to see the unnecessary, self-induced mess this country has gotten itself into. I think after I finish rambling, he would still have the "deer in the headlights look" and just say, "Well, if enough people in a country turn their back on God Almighty...."

He would probably trail off right there, as I've heard him do before. He had confidence that I was aware enough to not have to state the obvious. While I do have faith and believe in God, it *pales* in comparison to the level my Dad was at. As I have said before, "It was like it was part of his DNA."

For me, the saying, "I'm not worthy," comes to mind, referring to myself when compared to the level Dad was on. As I began this book, I was aware of a couple of spiritual occurrences like "A Touch of Heaven in Hell," where the bible falls out of his pocket and opens up to Psalms 23:4, "though I walk through the valley of the shadow of death……" *That* verse of all the verses it could have been. A Christmas story is another one but look at *all* the others. They are involved in every single incident that Dad was involved in, from the railroad story to getting captured. I am extremely pleased that this part of history can be passed on through my kids and grandkids, and they, too, will realize what a truly great human being my Dad was.

Also, the sacrifices the Greatest Generation gave for us to live free in peace and harmony and preserve our basic God-given human rights. I know all who read this book got a little boost in the areas of life that really matter. A boost in spirituality and faith, patriotism, love of country, and respect for all fellow Americans who share the same perspective and values. We *all* need this now more than ever. The greatest generation gave our generation the gift. Not only is it the greatest gift, it's the *only gift that matters.* This gift has *no* expiration date, and those who want to take it away from us will fail. It would be a sin to throw away our God-given liberties and freedoms that the greatest generation fought, sacrificed, and died for in order to pass on to us to a communist dictatorship.

We owe it to them as well as future generations. I feel that the *most* important purpose of this book is to teach our kids and future generations the *truth* about the heart of the USA and what makes it great. This book is *true* raw history that shows the good, bad, and ugly sides of war. We must learn from past history what keeps a nation strong and thriving. A strong military is a *must* for a nation to survive against foreign threats.

Remember, a bully only strikes when they sense weakness. The *only* way to win or discourage war *is peace through strength.* The most important thing by far is the leaders have common sense, a love for their country, and care about their people. Christian beliefs are the answers to a nation surviving against evil. When the ones at the top leading a nation turn their back on this as well as a proven, best-for-all constitution and are only fueled by power, hate, and self-enrichment at the expense of its own people, a nation will fall and fall hard. The worst thing that can happen to a country is for the people to divide and a war to break out within its own borders. The heart of America will not allow evil forces to take over this country. Who is that you ask? If you appreciate living in a country with liberties and freedoms, love your family, and respect all other Americans who share the same common-sense values and morals, *you* are the *heart* of America.

The way I see it, there is really no Democratic, Republican, left or right. There is common sense *good* and destructive *evil*. The ones who love our country far outnumber those who hate it and will preserve the gift, not only for us but for future generations to come.

OUR FREEDOM IS OUR GIFT

GOD BLESS THIS COUNTRY NOW AND FOREVER

ROBERT GILBERT

Ann & Roy Gilbert